All I Want is...
Everything

Tamara,

And the day came when the risk to remain tight in a bud was more painful than the risk it took to bloom!

Risk to become the beautiful flower I know you are!

With love, grace + gratitude!
Kim Bostone

All I Want Is...
Everything

A Guide To

Love, Peace and Happiness

By Kim Upstone

A New Day A New Vision, LLC. Publication

All I Want is...Everything: *A Journey to Love, Peace and Happiness.*

Copyright ©2009 Kim Upstone
Published by A New Day A New Vision, LLC.
Cover Design by Wenoah Rawlings

All rights reserved.

Reproduction or translation of any part of this work beyond that permitted by Section 107 or 108 of the 1976 United States Copyright Act without permission. Of the copyright owner is unlawful. Requests for permission or for further information Should be addressed to the Business Product Division,
A New Day A New Vision, LLC.

This publication is designed to provide accurate and authoritative information in regard to the subject matter covered. It is sold with the understanding that the Publisher is not engaged in rendering legal, accounting or other professional services. If legal advice or other expert assistance is required, the services of a competent professional person should be sought.

**Library of Congress Cataloging-In-Publication Data
is on file with the Library of Congress.**
ISBN-10: 0-984-0772-2-7
ISN-13: 978-0-984-0772-2-9

Contents

Acknowledgements	....	vii
My Gift to You	....	1
About Me	....	7
Finding You	....	17
Creating Your Map	....	33
Say It To Yourself	....	59
Your Beautiful Spirit	....	77
Choices	....	89
Gratitude	....	97
Happiness	....	105
Finding Love	....	121
Faith	....	137
The End But Never Done	....	145

In Gratitude

I wish to express my deepest gratitude to the following people who have helped make this book possible:

First and foremost I want to thank my husband. I will be eternally grateful for your love. It has been a gift beyond measure. Allowing me to grow in the light of my spirit, supporting me each and every step of our journey together.

I would like to thank my children for allowing me to practice my beliefs on them. I now know that allowing you to grow within the brightness of your own spirit has allowed you to flourish into wonderful individuals.

I would like to thank my sister Debbie for her patience and help.

I would like to thank my family and friends for the love that allowed me to find my way to the brightness.

I also want to thank Suzanne Jones for her patience and sharing my vision and Wenoah Rawlings for her creativity and belief that I would eventually find the right words.

And then with my deepest appreciation to my maker for allowing me to see my purpose in the brightness of the light.

My love and gratitude to you all!

Kim

My Gift To You

I believe there are no coincidences. In my heart I know that if you have this book in your hands you have it for a reason. Perhaps you came upon it by chance or a friend gave it to you. Maybe someone was speaking about it and you overheard the conversation. A power greater than you or I is at work. Maybe it is not meant for you but for someone you care about and you want them to have the happiness and joy in their life they deserve. Maybe by you reading it first, you will realize there are changes you can make to your life that will not only enrich your life, but will enrich the lives of everyone around you.

I look upon the journey I have taken as being as important to me as it is to everyone I have touched along the way. Each of us can benefit from making positive changes in our lives and that is why I am sharing my story with you. Some of you may be touched deeply by this book; and others will read it and take away small pieces for their journey. Some may find the timing is not right and will keep it in their stack of other unread books until the time is right. Still others will decide it is too risky to venture into the water without knowing what lies beneath the surface. Be unafraid and walk up to the water's edge. Consider dipping your foot in the water.

You may find your fear is unfounded and the things that are lurking below the surface that you have been afraid to face are not all that frightening once you face them. As painful as you fear it might be to begin this transformation, the happiness and joy you will experience will eclipse any uncertainty you feel along the journey. Similar to childbirth, it is easy to lose sight of the miracle that awaits but when that painful process is over and the miracle is in your hands, the memory of that pain fades until it is all but forgotten. There is no greater gift to give yourself than to live the rest of your time here with inner peace, joy and happiness. You have the power to unlock the invisible shackles that weigh us down and make life more of a chore than a celebration. You hold the key by deciding to take control and work towards recapturing the light within your spirit.

We all know the saying *"You are the only real problem you have, and you are the only real solution".* And it is very true. No one can take this journey for you; it is one voyage that everyone must take on their own.

Do you want to be one of the lucky few who know what it really means to live? Do you want to learn how to live without placing conditions on your life and allow happiness to fill your spirit? We all know the conditions we place on ourselves like: I will be happy when… I find love, lose weight, and have the house, car or the life depicted in my dreams. You must no longer keep happiness at bay waiting for the time when everything is perfect in your life, before allowing yourself to have *your everything*.

We will work through this process step by step. For this journey you will only need two things - a journal or notebook with lined pages and, most importantly, the belief that you are worth the effort to find the wondrous gifts that await you. You may need to read a chapter more than once before moving on to the next. Always do the work I ask of you as you move through the process. Even if you are uncomfortable writing down your thoughts and observations, look within and find the words to put on paper. They will be a true reflection of the progress you will make on this journey. Envision this process as walking up a long flight of stairs looking up from the bottom to the top seems far away. But, if you take the steps one at a time and rest when you tire, you will be at the top without even realizing you have climbed all that way. Each step will be one step closer to the happiness and peace you are searching for.

I can tell you with all the love in my heart that you too can have *"your everything"*. You have all that you need within yourself to find inner peace and it is not reliant upon external conditions. But please don't confuse being content with what you have, with not striving to have more. Human nature is to always look for something more which is why you are reading this book. Understand that there is nothing wrong with wanting more or better. The problem occurs when we make the absence of what we want and the lack of appreciation for what we have, exclusive of our own happiness. This is not a rehearsal for the life that we want, this IS your life so please read on and make the most of every moment of the gift of life we have been given.

My wish for each of you is that when we reach the end of this book together you will realize, as I have, the power in living each day with…

>…*love* for all and be able to truly love everyone including yourself without restrictions.

>…*grace* with gentleness towards others and acceptance of their limitations.

>…*and gratitude* for all that we have been given.

"*A life is like a piece of paper on which everyone leaves their mark*" – Chinese Proverb

All I Want Is Everything

My wish is that the mark I leave on your paper is one that will carry you to the end of the journey with the light of your spirit shining brightly and peace and contentment in your heart.

About Me

I had allowed the river to take me. And so it was that I was lost. We were traveling, on our way to a long needed vacation. Driving through the mountains, how perfect the picture appeared. My husband was quietly humming to songs on the radio and my children were asleep in the backseat. But at that moment I was once again overwhelmed with the feeling and the realization that with all I had, I really had nothing. My life seemed surreal, as if I was walking through it, as if it was all a dream. I felt alone even when surrounded by people. I was unconnected and lost and asking myself how did I get here. And even though I was asking the question in my head, my heart knew what I had done; I had let the river take me.

I had all these wonderful things. Things that you think would make you happy; wonderful husband and children, a house, cars, friends, family and faith. Wasn't that supposed to be all you needed to be happy? What was wrong with me? *All I wanted was everything,* but I had no idea what that everything was. Even more upsetting was the thought that I may never find that elusive something that would allow me to live consciously in every moment, and to feel love and gratitude for all that I had.

I must be missing something, some integral part that would allow me to be happy, to live in the moment, to look at all the things I had and allow them to be enough. Maybe I was born without that final piece to this complex puzzle, which is my life. Finding the missing piece would allow me to make sense of everything and make the puzzle complete. That missing piece must be the answer to everything. Where was it? Did I have it and lost it or was it always missing? Maybe those pieces no longer fit the puzzle because of all the other pieces from my life I had forced into those empty spots. Knowing they did not fit, but hoping I could somehow make the pieces come together and make me complete.

Maybe my search was in vain; maybe my puzzle would never be complete. My life had been anything but perfect and certainly not without drama. Drama created by me to make things more important than they were. Any distraction was a welcome one whether created or imagined. I must find a new path, the path I was on had never lead me to find the answers I needed. I had to try something new. Continuing to blame anyone including myself would not help me find what I was looking for to fill the emptiness within my spirit.

As I sat quietly in that car with thoughts spinning in my head, I realized that I seemed to be the only person who thought something was wrong. Was I that good at pretending? My husband and children were perfectly happy. I made their life as perfect and free from problems as I could – perhaps at a steep cost to myself. Sometimes I really wanted my husband to be as unhappy as I was, he shouldn't be happy he needed to share my pain.

My friends seemed to be happy without even the slightest hint that they knew how I felt or that they too were searching for something missing in their life. Looking back I realize that, no one could possibly have known how I felt, it was a well-guarded secret. Besides I wasn't supposed to be unhappy. To the outsider looking in I had *my everything*. Maybe my friends felt the same way as I; maybe we were all just keeping it to ourselves and playing the role we were supposed to play.

I read every book I could get my hands on, searching in vain for answers. Books that told me that I already had everything I needed, or to just figure it out, or better yet just do it. But do what? Where do you start when you can't even define what is wrong? Where do you look for happiness

About Me

when happiness in the world seemed to be defined by money and possessions? But I knew it wasn't there.

When I was busy the feelings would fade away. But when it was quiet my spirit would rise up from the dark and ask me why are you settling for this life without at least looking for what is missing. Where was that elusive piece of the puzzle that held the key to my completeness and my happiness? When I find it will the puzzle finally be complete?

How dare I ask to have it all? Who was I to expect everything? The questions kept guilt, my constant companion, always present in my mind. I have been given so much already. What do I have to complain about? So many people have problems and challenges far worse than mine. And even though I had allowed that river to take me where it chose, I was grateful that it had been a gentle ride so far. But until that moment while riding through the mountains I never considered that I had choices.

What would happen to me if the trip got bumpy? No one ever told me that I needed oars or even a map to help steer my life in a defined direction. But yet here I was in that boat on that river. Was I really ready to face the unknown and risk rocking the boat? I was always trying to keep everything steady and smooth afraid of all those questions I did not know the answer to. I didn't know how deep the water was or what was in the water. I may drown before I find all the answers.

I was tired of being imprisoned in the darkness. Over the course of many years I had occasionally seen glimmers of light from within. But I had no idea how to make the light brighter. I knew the sadness in my heart was from remaining in that darkness. , I had allowed myself to believe that if I could just forget that empty dark place within, maybe that feeling would just fade and I would just live the rest of my life in that darkness. But I knew I couldn't just give in, after years of keeping that overwhelming pain at bay. There was no other way. I must take the risk; I would drown alone in that darkness if I allowed myself to just be taken where that river would lead me.

I decided at that very moment, to risk it all and find a way to define what I really wanted from this life. I needed to define *my everything* and go after it. I would search for that missing piece that would fill my spirit with light. And as I sat there in the quiet I envisioned myself as the bud of a rose that refused to open remaining tight and safe. It would be the biggest risk of my life to bloom. As painful as it would be to face the unknown, the bud must take the risk. Either way the flower would eventually wilt and die; it might as well come to its end in full bloom with the petals falling one by one from its stem with all its energy being spent on becoming as beautiful as it was meant to be. I knew I must give every ounce of strength to bring joy to my life and maybe for a while allow those close to me to enjoy the glorious aroma and beauty of the flower as it blooms. The painful thorns on that rose which had been used to keep others at a distance were now just part of the risk those near to me must take to embrace me as I bloom.

I had decided; I must find what was missing. I was determined to find a way to make my spirit bright and to find real happiness and joy. And then in that moment, which I will never forget, something changed. I realized the heat of the sun was burning my arm and the knot I always felt in my stomach from the feelings I buried there, was gone. A wave of chills washed over my skin, something I had not felt in a very long time. I felt the heat of the sun and saw the beauty of the mountains and I was present in that very moment. Was the weight I had allowed to rest on my shoulders for years starting to release its grip?

I began to see that being part of the search for *my everything* would require that I become an active participant in my own life. Being part of the search for the dimmest of lights left within my spirit would be the first step in the journey that I now realize was the greatest gift I could have ever received. I understood that my entire life was a gift, with all of its joy and pain, beauty and ugliness. I am now aware that the pain is there to keep us searching for the answers making it more difficult to become complacent. And as I slowly moved out of the darkness, I eagerly embraced the light. I would eventually find the keys to unlock all the doors to embrace the wonder that would lie beyond the darkness. There is light beyond the darkness, I have seen it; I am living in it.

In the beginning, my purpose for writing this book was purely selfish because I was writing it only for me. But as I wrote I realized that maybe there was a larger purpose. Perhaps I was supposed to allow others a peek into my transformational journey in an effort to help them find peace and contentment and learn to how to brighten their spirit. Maybe part of my purpose in this life was to walk with you through the steps I took to find my way.

I hope by the end of the book you have learned how to put your oars in the water and to gently steer your boat in the direction that you choose, all the while enjoying the beauty that surrounds you on this journey. To have a destination in mind and not end up at the river's end and wonder sadly what did I do to get here? When in reality it is what you *failed to do* that chose your destination for you. I want you to take responsibility for your own life and begin your journey to find *your everything*.

About Me

I will guide you how to watch for those moments that are your gifts, as these are the only things that we take with us when this part of our journey is over. I will explain to you what you can do to define what you really want and show you how you can have *your everything*. You may be surprised at what you determine your heart's desires really are, and they may change as you set your course and your trip progresses. I will show you the path to appreciation and acceptance of things you can't change. Freeing yourself to become that beautiful flower, blooming for all to see.

I long to share my enlightenment with everyone who needs to rekindle the light in their spirit as much as I needed to. For me it was a long journey. However I am forever blessed that my spirit refused to settle for dimness. My life is now joyful and filled with gratitude and there is a sense of peace and love in my heart, and a light so bright in my spirit that it sometimes overwhelms me. This incredible happiness is something I want everyone to have.

When I embarked on this journey the search was to reclaim my brightness but it ended up brightening the lives of so many others. I still have a wonderful husband and children and parents. I have a great house and I still have things. But now I realize the things that I can't live without are free, not just things that can be purchased but things that I nurture within to brighten my spirit.

Many things have changed during this journey, mostly in me, and many things have not changed. I have learned to accept the things I cannot change and move on. I can now look back and say that the light, though dim, was still within and the piece I thought was missing was neither missing nor lost. Everything I thought was missing was still there hidden in a secret place safe from all the outside influences that bombard us daily and take their toll on our spirit. Once we learn to quiet ourselves we can hear what our heart is telling us from that secret place. We can hear our voice within, quietly telling us what our heart is saying and we can reclaim the light.

So join me on this journey and see what wonderful gifts your life holds. I will ask you to trust me and have faith that if you do the work consistently and honestly you will have the life you deserve. As you work step by step through the book you will become more and more aware of the beauty that surrounds you. You will begin to see and feel the difference everyday and your gifts will begin to appear before you. Quiet the noise and you will hear the song your heart sings.

Believe that the spirit within deserves to be nurtured and that you deserve to be loved. You will achieve balance and harmony within, no matter the circumstances that have come before. Believe that the light from your spirit, once brightened, will reward you with blessings that you can take with you when this part of the journey is complete.

Let's take the first step and look at *who* we really are…

Finding You

"Every decision you make – is not a decision about what you do. It's a decision about Who You Are. When you see this, when you understand it, everything changes. You begin to see life in a new way. All events, occurrences, and situations turn into opportunities to do what you came here to do". Neale Donald Walsch

It's all about you. I know your first response will be, "No it is not because I could never make it all about me!" I know it is hard to think in those terms but it *is* about you. Think about it. You are a wondrous gift, a gift from a higher power. You are the greatest gift you have ever been given and if you think of yourself as unimportant you will never find the happiness you deserve. It really is all about you and as you continue this journey you will see why it is vitally important to understand and acknowledge it.

Think of yourself as a light. If you feel that your light has dimmed, or that you are living in the dark, you need to find out how to turn that light back on. One of the most valuable lessons I learned during my journey is that I am the only one that can turn on the light within or make it shine brighter. And the only way to figure out how to keep the light burning brightly was to focus on me.

The power to keep that light shining brightly comes from the needs of your spirit being continually replenished and reenergized. Your light is a gift and when it is shining bright and strong, you will not be able to keep it to yourself. You will want to share it with everyone and help illuminate the world. However, you cannot share your light what you do not have. So first we must find your light.

Finding the light will take work but there is no limit to its brightness once found. I think as we age we expect and allow the light within to dim. Some of us have seen our parent's lights dim and assume that same fate awaits us. The light dims because we are not being aware. We give ourselves over to the river; and are in that boat unaware, fading into the sunset of our lives. I promise you, that this is not as it was intended! We need to work to keep our light bright and strong. We need to put in the time and effort to figure out how to keep it shining brightly. That is where we will begin our journey.

Who are you? Good question! I am not asking what you are – wife-mother-daughter-sister but rather who you are. We spend no time thinking about who we are in relation to the world around us. As babies it doesn't matter who we are we just know we are. The world revolves around us and we are very good at making our wants and needs known. We know instinctively who we are and that we are deserving of having those needs fulfilled.

As we get older we begin to relate to the world around us a little bit differently. We find our place and make our needs fit into the place we are in. We are told we are selfish if we put our wants and needs first. We are expected to put them aside for the happiness and comfort of others. We spend time working on relationships with parents, friends, lovers, spouses and children and try to ignore what we need to make our own spirit bright.

What we inadvertently end up doing is depleting our spirit of the power and energy it needs to shine brightly. By abandoning what we need, we allow the wants and needs of others to gradually fill in the hole that develops in our spirit. Their dependency upon us fills that hole for a short time while giving us a false belief that we are living a rich and fulfilled life. But it is not our life. As our own light fades we begin to feel like we are drowning. In desperation we cling to others expecting them to be the light for us instead of remembering that we know how to keep our own light bright.

As the years pass and you continue to abandon the notion that your wants and needs are vital to keep the light shining brightly, the light continues to dim. Your reasoning is that people need you or do you actually need them? By sacrificing your needs, without even realizing it, you have set up unrealistic expectations for others.

No one can keep your light bright but you and although a candle loses nothing by lighting another candle, you cannot keep another candle burning brightly by dimming yours. In an effort to keep your spirit whole and bright you begin to expect or demand certain behaviors or actions from others to keep even the dimmest light visible in your spirit. But even the dimmest of lights peeking through, will remind us that the light, no matter how dim, is still present.

Living vicariously through others, making their problems yours, demanding proof of loyalty and love are all ways to keep control and the empty space in your spirit filled. You have set yourself and others up for failure for not living up to what you want them to do and be. Your expectations, your wants and your needs are being fulfilled through them. Setting up such expectations for yourself and others only closes off any chance of happiness unless you receive the expected results to fulfill your expectation every time. Disappointment and unhappiness soon become the norm and the dimness of the light within becomes so comfortable you forget what it feels like to be bright, and truly happy.

People you are close to grow tired of having to be something that they are not; weary of trying to fill the empty spot in your spirit. They become trapped in a never-ending quest to be the catalyst for someone else's peace and happiness. For some, the search to keep the light bright can turn destructive looking for answers in indulgence in food, drinking, drugs, and spending. These destructive behaviors all stem from the never-ending search for contentment and happiness.

Believe me when I tell you *everything* you need to be happy is free. Peace in your heart, the love you give to others, and the love you receive from family and friends are all free. Your hopes, dreams, relentless spirit and the ability to choose to look with gratitude at your gifts are in themselves the priceless gifts that we forget we possess. These gifts are what keep the light in our spirit bright. They are the real gifts possessed by everyone the world over.

We may occupy a certain position in this world and wonder how it is that someone with what we consider less than us can be happy. Some of the poorest countries in the world have the happiest people. How can this be? It is because they too have the free gifts but their view is not clouded by possessions. They recognize that things you buy cannot bring lasting happiness. Possessions cannot bring real lasting joy to your heart. Food, alcohol and drugs can numb us for a while, but they cannot brighten a spirit dimmed.

To find peace and contentment you need to get rid of the idea that money in any amount will be the answer. It will not. Be aware that some of the wealthiest countries have the unhappiest people. Money allows many physical comforts but it cannot make your journey to find peace, happiness and contentment easier. These need to be earned by hard work and reflection. You will end your journey with what you began with – the free gifts we have all been blessed with and that reside within our hearts. And we are foolish to not live everyday with gratitude for having been given them.

Becoming clear about where you are now and where you want to be, will make the journey ahead easier. We will not spend time looking back. You cannot move forward while looking in the rear view mirror. It is much easier to see the vast openness of the road looking forward at the horizon and envisioning the unlimited opportunities for happiness that lie in front of you.

We all know that rowing against the flow of the river just tires you and eventually you will give in and go with the flow again. The same applies when you relive past experience over and over in your mind. That destructive behavior creates no momentum to move forward - it just makes you weary and tired. Surrendering to the scars on your spirit does nothing to move them out of the way to make room for the brightest of lights. I am sure some of you reading this have had terrible experiences that may feel impossible to overcome. If you feel you truly cannot move past them than you need to seek professional help.

Whether you seek out other books or counseling you deserve the opportunity to learn how to get beyond the darkness in your spirit. If you choose to continue on this journey with me you must look forward. The darker your life has been, the brighter even the dimmest light will look. A candle that has remained in the dark has the same brightness as a candle in a room filled with light. But the candle in the dark appears brighter because there has been no other light around it. Your chances for peace and contentment are just as good as another person who has not had such challenging experiences.

A very important part of our enlightenment is to become AWARE. Becoming aware will be one of your most useful tools on this entire journey. Write the word AWARE at the top of your first page of your journal. We will refer to this word many times during each day. It will be the first step in bringing ourselves back towards the light from where ever we find ourselves now.

Before beginning this journey with me you may want to think about how this journey will be perceived by others. I recommend caution in telling people that you are beginning this journey with me. If you announce to friends and family that you are changing and you don't care what anyone thinks about the changes, you may create resistance. They will not understand when you explain, "I am finding the light in my soul that has gone dim" and they may not be especially supportive. Realize that this transformation is about you and you alone. Some people may even become defensive and attempt to analyze everything you do. They may resist every change they see in you because they like the way things are now or are afraid of any change.

Think of yourself as being a pebble tossing yourself into the water and creating tiny ripples. These ripples softly and peacefully lull our friends and loved ones. And as we make gentle, subtle changes to ourselves while they hardly notice.

Let's start by looking at who we are. I asked you earlier and you may have thought you didn't need to think about your answer. When I began my journey I had no idea who I was, as you read in the previous chapter I was lost. I could not have accurately described who I was, or even the specific point in time where I became lost to myself.

So who are you? At this point, you may be confused about what exactly I am looking for. Understand that you won't know who you are until you reach the point where you do not need others to reinforce who you think you are; or require acknowledgement or admiration from anyone. You will not need conditions to be perfect for you to brighten your light. Only then will you be able to really know who you are.

I can tell you who I am now but I will save that for further on. Some of you will be able to create a list of who you think you are. Good for you but you still need to do the work outlined in this chapter. You may be so much more than you think you are; or you may find you are not exactly who you think you are. You may think of yourself as ordinary and not deserving. I can tell you that you are very wrong.

Some of you will be like me and simply not have a clue. Either way at this point we will start to look for who we want to be by spending a few days with your journal. You will need to be quieter than normal for the next few days. I want you to concentrate on observing and listening to others and become AWARE. Read on to see how we will accomplish this.

We are now at the first step on the staircase moving towards the light. Visualize yourself placing your foot on that first step. We will begin our journey by observing how others speak to you and listen carefully to what they say. Just listen to spouses, children, coworkers, bosses and even strangers and write down the words they speak to you in your journal. If you feel that their words are hurtful, put an * by the words in your journal. Or, if their words evoke a good feeling put a ! next to the words. You don't need to write everything that is said, but make sure to write down any phrases that evoke emotion in you.

Write them down exactly how they are said word for word and who said them. Do this for at least two days during the week and over a weekend. You should encounter most of the people you normally would in your everyday life. This is a very important exercise and four days is the minimum to establish a pattern. Keeping your journal near you at all times makes it easier. Call family, friends or people you normally speak to on the phone just to say hi. Call people who previously have brought out feelings of emotion in you. Remember you are a pebble. Do not instigate or start trouble just to hear the words they use.

When you think you have a good mix of people and a decent list of conversations you are ready for the next step.

If you are tempted to read on without completing the list, please stop and finish the work. I understand there are those of you who are just too curious and will read on. I believe you will be more open to what is said to you and not have preconceived notions about what we are looking for. We are at the point of choice and as always it is your choice. So you can put the book away until you have finished the work to reap the most benefit, or you can read on to the end of the chapter.

Thank you for finishing the journaling if you did, but either way we are ready to move on. Let's look at the all the ! points in your journal these are the words that made you feel good. How many conversations written are from people you respect and admire for their integrity and honesty, and whom you trust and feel have your best interest at heart? Put a big heart by them. This is fabulous even if you only have one - it is a start! If you have none, we need to look at who you are choosing to surround yourself with which we will talk about in the chapter ahead called Choices.

Now let's look at the * items. How many of those are from people you respect and admire? Do they represent admirable qualities? Are they caring and loving and have

27

your best interest at heart? Cross off any words that came from anyone other than those people. You are the only one who knows what you are doing so be brutally honest. Some of the words you cross off may have come from close family members. The only items left on your list should be from those people you have chosen to allow to be an influence on your life. Look at the words that are remaining. Were you interpreting their words correctly? Were their words spoken in a moment of their darkened spirit? Reflect upon the situation at the time you wrote it down. When people we respect and admire say something that affects us, we need to examine their intention, and look at what was said. Then make a choice decide to embrace it as something we may need to change within ourselves, or reject it as something that was said in a moment of anger or emotion.

What about the words I had you cross off things said from the rest of the people? I can honestly tell you I don't give a moment's thought to what people I don't respect and admire say to me and you shouldn't either. This sounds harsh but you'll quickly become adept at dismissing words from those people as you become more and more aware. If you absorb all the negativity these people throw your way it will not allow you to be who you want to become. You will never find *your everything*!

As we take this journey and your spirit becomes filled with inner peace and happiness you will realize that nothing anyone says or does, can impact the light in your spirit unless you allow it. Decide right now who you respect and admire, and who is important in your life. Let everyone else be what they want to be. Do not give them any space in your mind or spirit. We do not need to change everyone else to be able to change ourselves. The only person you can change is you. By making the changes to strengthen your spirit, you can be the light they may choose to embrace. Either way it is their choice. They are responsible for themselves.

I found as I stopped allowing their words to affect me, that there was an escalation in their attempt to draw me into a confrontation. Because I was now aware of what was occurring, by simply acknowledging what they said with "do you really think so" or "that's an interesting way to look at it". But by refusing to comment and be drawn into an exchange or by simply changing the subject they soon tire of trying to drag you along in the conversation and simply leave you alone. It is not as much fun for their ego when you don't play the game with them and they will move on to easier prey.

Now I need to clarify one vitally important point. Everyone is responsible for themselves, but there is one exception and that is our children. We are responsible for any life we bring into this world. Even very young children can learn about choices and being responsible for those choices. There is no greater gift for us to give to our children then the right to their own self-enlightened bright spirit. By learning how to keep our own spirit bright, we free them to learn how to keep their spirit bright by their own self-love.

Giving our children, the gift of self-love and helping them to nurture their own spirit builds a self-reliant adult. An adult who can enter into a relationship free from conditions and expectations and build one of admiration and respect for others – all of which is vital for their lifelong happiness. Raising children is a daunting task but is much easier if we take this journey and emerge from the darkness ourselves enlightened with a light bright enough to light even the darkest teenage years.

Turn to a new page in your notebook because we are moving on but we will need to take with us what we have just learned. We need to be aware of the things that are said to us and aware that we have a choice on what we will allow ourselves to absorb into our minds. If you were not able to complete this step you should not move on. Do the exercise until it becomes clear which people in your life you will allow to influence you. When you feel strong enough to resist the negativity from others then you can move on. Remember this is not a race if you want the change to be lasting and life changing. Understand that it may take time to be able to make the necessary changes necessary. Please don't give up but understand that we each truly deserve happiness and love unconditionally.

I will tell you now who I am. I am a gift to myself. I am the light in my spirit and the voice singing in my heart. I am love, joy and happiness and when I say those words out loud they tickle my heart and soul. These are things that others did not give me. These are not things others need to acknowledge within me for me to know they are there. There was no cost to me for these things. These are gifts that make my light shine bright and strong.

Come with me and let's create our map to our *everything*...

Creating Your Map

"Do not fear that your journey will someday end but rather that it will never begin".

Author Unknown

Let's walk together conscious of this glorious journey we are on. Developing an awareness and appreciation of all the joy and beauty that is around you at every moment is not an easy task, but is essential to your spirit becoming and remaining bright. The constant toll that we pay for living a busy life is apparent when we look at the light in our spirit. One event after another fills your time with seemingly insignificant matters and these events demand your attention and distract you from things that make your spirit bright. These events deprive you of that awareness of the beauty that surrounds you.

You must work each day to look for the moments of happiness and joy or they will blend in and be lost in the haste to make it to the next event. Moving too fast allows life to become a blur. We each must take the time to stop and realize that we are here not merely to exist but to live

Creating Your Map

every moment with clarity and consideration of each choice offered to us. You must look for those choices aware of the effect they have upon you and your spirit. Once you recognize and accept that you have choices to make and that those choices will empower and strengthen you, then you have found a tool vital to finding *your everything*.

Let's begin to create a direction to move in, a compass for you to take with you on the journey. We will use this compass daily to help us stay close to our true destination, with the intention firmly rooted in our mind of determining who we want to be.

Let's look at how we normally prepare for a trip. You choose a destination, map out an intended route, determine what you need to take with you, and you have a good idea where you need to end up. You may make small adjustments along the way but you have an understanding of what you need to do to reach your destination. You trust that the trip will be relaxing and enjoyable because you have prepared. You're confident that you have everything you need for your trip. Now you can relax and enjoy the trip taking pleasure in the beautiful scenery all around you and in the journey itself.

However, until now you have been on the most important journey of your life, with no compass or map. You may have a destination in mind, but no idea how to get there and when you eventually reach the end of the river, will you have enjoyed the journey? You stepped into that boat without giving much thought about this journey you are on every day, the journey that encompasses the entirety of your existence here.

The river has chosen your path for you and you have just gone along for the ride. What if you hit a patch of really rough water? Would you just hold onto the sides and wait for it to be over? What if you were to hit the rough water over and over again? Would you be content to just hold on again and again, just waiting for that rough part to be over? Or would you rather choose to do a little preparation, make some choices and then relax and enjoy the journey? Understand that the choices you make now will increase the chances that you will not miss the happiness and joy along the way - regardless of rough water.

Our map and our compass will be our guide taking us in the direction we choose to go. You may decide to alter your original course or use the oars to slow down a bit. But all the while you know that you are headed in the direction that *you* have chosen.

My intention in having you create a map is not to have you define every step. That would establish unrealistic expectations and create unhappiness if not fulfilled. Realizing each step we take will be a transformational experience we may need to adjust our course slightly along the way. A map that we create today may differ slightly from one we would create further into our journey. What will not change is our destination and who we want to become. You will find an awakening to peace and contentment, a life where happiness is allowed free of conditions.

No one will know better than you, after reflection, where you want to go or who you want to be. To find those answers you need to your ask your heart for guidance. To return the light to your spirit you need to look deep inside to your heart's desires. Desires not of possessions, which will cloud your perspective, but the desires that will lead you towards *your everything*.

The map you create will allow you to become aware, think with clarity and find answers to your questions. Your journey may be easier if you can spend time with the people who you know are bright spirited or those that support or inspire you. It will be easy to locate those people bright of spirit because you will be naturally drawn to their brightness. They possess what you are seeking - an inner calm that radiates, grace and happiness. These are people that you will carefully listen to when they speak.

Even though this journey is one you take alone, it will be more difficult if you surround yourself with people who are dark spirited or light stealers, who will attempt to seek out and steal any brightness within your spirit. Your process of moving towards brightening your own light will allow you to better recognize the darkness of spirit in some and the brightness of spirit in others. You will eventually learn how to discern between the two. For now please use caution around people with dark spirits. They will be the people who want to share their unhappiness with everyone including you. I am not saying to avoid all people with dimness or darkness in their spirits, which would be impossible, just know that once your spirit is bright and strong you will be compelled to share that brightness. But for now learning to distinguish between the two, and how they affect you and your own brightness, is important.

We will never avoid everyone who has a dark spirit, but when you are making your way towards the light, you need to be completely aware of who near you has darkness of spirit. These are people who will take every opportunity to share their darkness and try to entice you wander off your path. They are completely happy with living their life in this darkened state and see no reason to change. Sadly, they live completely unaware of the joy within their reach. Hopes and dreams for them are not treasures; they don't even realize all that is hidden in their darkness. Love is merely a

Creating Your Map

word they use, not a feeling that lives in the deepest recesses of their heart. Gratitude is foreign to them as they do not know how to express or feel gratitude. So, for now, avoid interacting with these people as much as possible.

At this step in my journey I often found myself becoming angry at this type of person. I was becoming bright of spirit, changing my view, why couldn't they? I simply couldn't understand why they were so uninterested in holding a conversation that did not involve negativity and why they had nothing to add when I tried to make the discussion bright and enlightening. Awareness allowed me to realize that my anger was drawing me off the course I was setting. I was practicing the negative self-talk we will soon learn about and I was allowing it to clutter my mind with "whys".

I was looking in the rear view mirror instead of looking to the horizon, which was the direction I needed to travel to reach *my everything*. I recognized the negative person I was now angry with was me prior to beginning my own journey. Awareness of what I was doing allowed me to look at and realize that it was my ego from which I was viewing the encounters. In judging others, I was allowing my ego to compare my state with that of another. Creating a 'I am right' and 'they are wrong' scenario in my mind, which serves no purpose. Seeing it from my spirit's perspective allowed me to switch my anger to compassion. By removing my judgment of them, I realized they were not aware of their spirit's darkness and negativity. Awareness on my part brought clarity to the situation.

You have now had a few days to practice turning off the noise from others. Having completed your first journaling assignment we can now move forward aware of what we are allowing others to place into our mind. Are you beginning to realize the impact of what people say and how it influences you? Can you see the harm done by embracing everything that is said to you?

You will soon be able to unconsciously weed out what you will allow in and what you will dismiss without even a second thought. Care should be taken that you don't dismiss everything just because it is not what you want to hear. It is a fine line to walk but be honest with yourself and be aware that each encounter is an opportunity to be attentive. Remain vigilant, and be a filter for what you allow to reach your mind and spirit.

Are you ready to move to the next step? Do you understand how filling your head with everything that is said dims your spirit? If you feel you are ready, step up so both feet are on the next stair. Once you are there look around. You have only moved up one step but you are a world away from where you were.

Creating Your Map

Can you see in your mind that landing below, slightly darker and filled with all the words you have discarded over the past days? Visualize a pile of dark words that you did not allow to affect you and your being. Feel very proud of yourself, this is not an easy step to take. Stop for a few moments and enjoy the realization that you are now on your way. Your journey has truly begun.

This entire process will take time. We live in an instant gratification society where we want everything immediately. Working on personal development and waiting as the process unfolds can be a daunting task. When we are used to getting everything we want quickly, things that take time can be discouraging. For my journey I found that by doing daily journaling allowed me to more easily remain on my path. I became ever more aware of how those around me affected my spirit which gave me motivation to not abandon the process. I realized that I needed to work consistently for the results to be lasting and life changing.

The time it takes for you to nurture your spirit back to brightness cannot be rushed. Remember to rest at each step before attempting the next. This is not a race to the top nor does the one with the quickest time win. Each step we take will be a different timetable for every person. This process is about giving ourselves a gift of the time we need to find our *everything*, there is no need to rush. If you are not ready simply keep working on step one and when you are ready feel free to move on. But you must keep working towards finding *your everything*. You must not stop and become complacent or you will lose momentum.

On the search you may encounter resistance from others for making changes that affect their world. Say to yourself before continuing on, "I cannot now, or ever be, the *everything* for other people. As much as I love my family and friends and want to make everything perfect for them, this is a journey that we each must travel on our own. We must each find the strength within to search out answers to make our spirit bright". What we each must learn from this transformation will be slightly different. So it is truly a journey we take alone.

What can you do to remain vigilant staying in the light of who we want to become instead of becoming who others see us as? Realizing that if I don't recognize all the beauty that resides within me I will just assimilate others' definitions of who I am, into who I become. There is no brightness in becoming what others define you as. Brightness comes from the self awareness of the wondrous gift that you are, as you begin to ask the questions to define, create and become the light yourself.

Creating Your Map

Are you ready to begin? If you are ready, let's continue on our journey. Get your journal out and get ready for the second step. Let's create our vision of ourselves.

It is important that you properly prepare for each group of questions you will find throughout the remainder of this book. For each upcoming session you will need to find some quiet time to work. The questions listed in each session should not be completed all at one time. Take time whenever possible. Some of you will be tempted to move quickly through the questions but please resist the temptation. Spend time allowing each question to linger in your mind. Each group of questions may take a day or days to complete. Working in a quiet environment may seem strange because we are so used to background noise but the quiet will make it easier to calm yourself and listen to the voices inside. Take your journal and when ready read through the questions within each session. Write your answers to those questions but before beginning turn your paper sideways writing across the lines. Don't worry about grammar or punctuation. Writing across the lines side to side might make you a little uncomfortable but this is what we want. We need to feel a bit uneasy to reach outside of the confines of our old views. Try to align your heart and mind by being honest with yourself.

Look at the questions within each chapter and reach deep inside for your answers. They can contain anything that comes to your mind. Do not edit at this time. Don't worry if you are having trouble finding the place within where your secret desires reside. Your spirit has been denied focused attention for so long you may not be able to reach into its depths right now. Just write a word that relates to your journey and then expand from there. Try writing in your journal at different times of the day.

I found that my best time to write was when I was weary or tired. It seemed that when my "happy face" defense was down it allowed me to get closer to those true feelings and nearer to that place within that held my secret desires. Try not to write when you have had caffeine. Caffeine may lessen the effect of the right brain and will make it easier to be logical with each answer. The questions I will ask you to answer all through our journey need to be answered emotionally. Avoid working on this when you are angry. There is darkness within us, when we are upset or angry that expands and completely drowns out what the heart and spirit are saying. The words we are looking for whisper to us while anger is very loud. Anger will always win so wait until you are no longer angry to do the work. If you do not wait, the result will be that of your ego's darkness and not the desires of your spirit.

Creating Your Map

Looking ahead to create a picture of who we want to be at the end of our journey will give us tremendous insight and a deeper understanding into who we need to become along the way. Know that you are extraordinary and in being the precious gift that you are, do not settle for less than your most profound vision of who you can be.

Look at the questions below and answer each truthfully. Not with what you think you should put down but with answers drawn from your spirit. Who do you want to become? If it is a very rich person with lots of possessions write that down. If you want to play golf on your last day on earth write that down. If you want to find inner peace and happiness write it down. If you want *everything*, define what *your everything* is. But try to reach down deep and be honest. You are the only person who will read this so locate your real self, and be true to that person.

1) *Who do I want to become?*
2) *If I had only one day left on earth how would I spend it?*
3) *Write down four words you would like to aspire to.*
4) *What is most important in my life?*
5) *What brings me the most joy and happiness?*
6) *What am I most grateful for in my life?*

Write the first question in your journal – remember write sideways across the lines of the page. Write the second question on the next page until you have pages for each of the six questions. Begin writing down thoughts and words that come to mind and then expand upon them. Take your time until you feel the answers reflect your true feelings. Let the answers surface from your heart. When you are comfortable with your answers we can move on together.

I know some of you will again read ahead. As with the previous chapter please put the book down and complete the questions. With this exercise it is even more important not to read ahead. Just select a few words from your answers to each question that best describe your deepest wishes. Fill in each blank in the next section with the words pulled from each of your answers. Write out the paragraph as you fill in the blanks.

> Wouldn't everyone want a life filled with joy and happiness, contentment touched their spirit wouldn't you have wanted to be like (your name)_____ . They worked hard their entire life to be _____. On their last day on this earth they spent their time_____. Everyone would love such a rich rewarding life and strives to be as _____ , _____ and _____ but

Creating Your Map

    most of all _____. Everyone knew what was most important in (your name)_____'s life and no matter the circumstances _____ always came first. Everyone knew what brought (your name) _____the most joy and happiness was _____. They lived each day with so much gratitude for _____.

Remind yourself that it doesn't matter what anyone else thinks, is this who you are or who you want to be? Read it again. Are you comfortable that it reflects your deepest wishes?

You have just written your own eulogy. If your answers were filled with references to anything but the gifts of your spirit, your heart, you were not successful in finding the place within your heart where your answers should have been set free from. You have choices at this point. You can stop and wait until you progress to the point in your life where you are ready to acknowledge that something other than possessions will bring you joy. Or, you can work very hard at being aware that there are so many more than things to own, and that the transformation that awaits will require you to search for something much more meaningful. Working hard now may allow you to achieve the balance needed to live in the material world and at the same time realize and appreciate your most valued possessions. Once you make this realization you will be able to apply the same appreciation of your outer external life as you will make to your spirit's brightness. You will find that your entire conscience changes. You will be propelled into this wondrous journey where you will view everything in your life with wonder and gratitude.

Let's review the questions and delve a little bit deeper into our thought process so that we become more aware and can make the changes needed.

The first question was - **Who do I want to become?** We may not have a clear picture yet of who we want to be but we all know someone we admire and wish we could emulate. That person may have a quality we admire like bravery, compassion, strength or generosity or an endless depth of peace and happiness.

When you think of these admirable qualities you may feel envious. Envy is when we admire the person who possesses a certain quality that we also would like to possess. Envy is quite different from jealousy. Jealousy requires that you want something that another person possesses, but at the same time you wish that they did not possess that particular quality. You want it only for yourself.

Creating Your Map

Do you see the difference? Envy involves no harmful feelings directed at another person, but jealousy aims destructive thoughts directly at the person. In the end, whose spirit does this harm? Yours!

I believe that admirable qualities evoke only envy and not jealousy because inherently we know we already possess these qualities. They may be lying dormant, or we have never been tested to see if we possess them, or perhaps we have not looked inside ourselves for them. However when we discuss wealth, riches and possessions people often think differently. This is where jealousy takes over and you lose sight of what is really important to possess.

Watch closely for jealousy on your journey and avoid it at all costs because it will take you further from your destination.
When you begin to feel jealous ask yourself:

- Why am I feeling like I want what they have?
- Would I give up everything to have it?
- If I had it would I feel complete and happy and would I never want for another thing?

You can certainly have possessions but you must keep them in perspective. Things you want should be things you need; they must be purpose driven; and they should never be acquired for the intention of being a reflection of *who* you are. For example, if you want a new car it should be because you *need* a new car or simply want a new car. You work hard and you deserve to have things that you want.

However, you should *never* purchase a new car because your friends are getting a new car, or you think it will result in true happiness. The feeling that you receive from that car will fade but the financial cost will remain. More importantly, there is a steep cost to your spirit. When you drive it, you may mistakenly believe it represents who you are but it does not. When you don't receive the expected adulation from it you may become disappointed and even angry. Finally, the jealous people with spirits that are dimly lit aren't really happy for you. They just want what you have and the cycle begins again. Soon there will be something else to want because the feeling it brought to you has not filled the empty space within. Remember, you can possess anything you want just be sure you do not confuse the things you have with who you are or who it will make you.

The second question was - **If I only had one day left on earth what would I do with it?** Look at your answer. I hope that you really thought about the question before answering it. How would you spend your last day? If you said something like play golf, work or decide what possessions you will leave to people in your will, think again. Are you really ready to continue reading this book and make life-altering changes? Did you spend your last day working on something you could take with you? Were love and gratitude your companion as you stood on the bank of the river? Did you nurture your spirit by sharing your love for others? Do you need to rethink your initial answer? Do you realize how grateful you might be to know when your last day would be so you could tell everyone how much they have meant to you? Should you start thinking like everyday will be your last? Take your answer and incorporate it into the map we will create as something that you need to be aware of as you progress on your journey.

The third directive was - **Write down four words you would like to aspire to**. I hope they were words that inspire you and you keep foremost in your mind when you are on your journey. I would hope that your words would originate from the depths of your heart. Words whispered from who you are becoming.

The fourth question was - **What is most important in my life?** This is a question only you can answer. Please give this one much reflection. Do you know what is most important? If you know what is most important are you making it your top priority? Are you giving it the attention the most important thing should be receiving? Many times the people we love and care about, and those who love and care about us, do not get the best part of us. There are many reasons why this may happen and when your spirit brightens it will be easier to share your gifts with everyone. For now be aware that the direction we are moving in requires we acknowledge what is most important in our lives.

The fifth question was - **What brings me the most joy and happiness?** How far are you away are you from remembering what brings joy and happiness to your heart? Are you happy now? Do you know what joy really feels like? When is the last time that you laughed? Has the heaviness in your spirit cast darkness over you? We were put on this earth to be a wondrous gift. We cannot allow ourselves to forget how it feels to be joyous and happy without placing conditions. You deserve to find the path back to *your everything* and that includes happiness.

Creating Your Map

The sixth question was - **What am I most grateful for?** Please make it something other than a car, house or job. We need to be grateful for our gifts. We need to appreciate the love of one another, peace and serenity in our hearts, happiness, hopes, dreams and even the ability to be grateful. Material possessions can all be taken away in a moment with only a memory left behind. Your free gifts, once acknowledged, will always be with you and can never be taken away.

Pick up your pen again and begin writing your journey's desires. If you feel lost look at the questions you answered above and the ones listed below. Write sideways across the lines again margin to margin keeping in mind this map is also your life's mission statement.

Before starting your map think through the picture you will be creating in your mind. Close your eyes and picture a beautiful day with the sun shining and white puffy clouds floating by. You are sitting in your boat on the river. The water is crystal clear, beautiful flowers line the banks of the river, and as the breeze blows lightly, trees create gently moving reflections and shadows on the surface of the water. You are alone in the boat but you don't feel alone. You are at complete peace.

You have embraced every moment of your life's journey and your heart overflows with love as it creates a beautiful glow all around you. Within the glow is the love you have given to yourself and the love you have freely given to others. This love surrounds and comforts you, and your spirit radiates with the knowledge that you are now one with the light. You are so grateful that you decided to not settle but continued to look for *your everything*. With the oars in your hands you can choose to gently slow down to fully enjoy the beauty or steer closer to the shore. But you can now be at peace because you know you have a choice. You have never felt this peaceful before and you know that you have changed. Open your eyes and feel the calm inside.

This is what you are now working towards. Search for these same feelings everyday in your life. Relate this feeling to your map. Be aware of the beauty around you at every moment. This is the place within you can return to at anytime, the place you need to find to feel at peace, every day. Know and understand that it is all within your reach.

It is time to create your map.

I will give you direction but you must create your map yourself. I have shared my map at the end of this chapter but only read it if you have trouble creating yours. Make

Creating Your Map

sure to write it as if you have already achieved *your everything*. Use the following reminders to keep you aware and to get to where you want to be. Let these statements guide your words as you begin to write.

I realize that I have _____

I will make time each day for _____

I will give myself the gift of _____

I have shown others _____

Today I was aware of _____

I see myself _____

As you write, keep in mind this is a compass not a turn-by-turn map. You may want to add to it all along our path to enlightenment and again when we near the end of this part of our journey. Return to this section for a daily vision of who you will become when you are standing at the end of the river.

Now it is time to write your personal mission statement.

Refer back to my direction on preparing to write in your journal. For now continue writing across the lines and be aware of the most favorable time to look into your heart for answers. Search to find the person that stands bathed in the light at the river's end. Visualize the person you want to become.

The following is my compass, which gives me direction every day. I read it every day and although I can revise it anytime I need to, I have changed it very little since I first wrote it 20 years ago.

I realize that I have allowed life and the river to sweep me past too many beautiful opportunities for happiness and joy during my journey, but I am determined to slow down and look everyday for those special moments. I will make time today to reflect upon my choices and on how I've spent my time. Are the choices I made today a true reflection of what I know is most important? Have I given myself the respect I deserve? Have I shown myself compassion and patience and spoken kindly to myself and others? Today I will close my eyes and look at my spirit light to make sure it is burning brightly and if I have allowed someone to dim it, have I given thought on how not to let that happen again? Have I been aware today of the dimness in others spirits and then looked with gratitude for the brightness within and for all the gifts I have acknowledged within myself?

Creating Your Map

As I move further along, continuing the journey on the river every day I am growing in the light and feeling more peace and contentment in my heart. I see myself now nearing the end of this part of my journey; on the shore I stand bathed in the light and warmth of my spirit. I am filled with the memories of all the joyous moments the sum of which is the life I have lived. I am embraced by the love I have given and received. I have no regrets only gratitude that I have not let the river take me where it chose but that I am now who I have chosen to be. I am ready for whatever the next journey has to hold, blessed to have lived in the light. I have been true to my heart. I have acknowledged the everything I was looking for was already within me and in finding my everything I was able to

… truly love everyone including myself without restrictions

…have grace with gentleness towards others and their limitations

…and show gratitude for the gifts I have discovered within myself.

I will live each and every day filled with love, grace and gratitude.

After finishing your map, please read it daily, allow it to be your compass, and guide you. You are becoming the person you were meant to be, the gift to yourself.

Now let's move forward with a better understanding of *who* we want to become using our map to guide our steps.

Say It To Yourself

"When there is no enemy within, the enemies outside cannot hurt you".

African Proverb

This next step involves making you aware of the conversation within your mind. What you say and think to yourself has a profound effect on your spirit and the level of peace and contentment you will allow yourself to achieve. We can be our own worst enemy when we fail to edit what we say to ourselves. What people say to you is completely out of your control. How you receive what was said, and what you say to yourself, is completely under your control.

Maybe your parents said something hurtful to you as a child that has remained with you. Or, perhaps a spouse, friend or coworker told you something that was cruel or unkind. Regardless of the source, you have held on to that hurt for a long time and it has prevented you from moving forward and becoming who you want to become. You continue to play what was said over and over in your mind.

Say It To Yourself

What is the real problem? You are. Where is the answer to the problem? In your head! More than likely these people forgot what they said long ago. Yet, there are some people whose ego would take great joy in knowing that what they said caused you to change the course of your journey.

I could spend a lifetime analyzing what motivates people to do and say certain things but it will do nothing to move us in the direction we need to go. I believe their spirit is dim and I can only hope they decide to choose a path that will brighten their journey. I have chosen long ago to not allow others to dim the light in my spirit and to not allow them one moment in my consciousness. I deny them any attention and I hope by reading and understanding the concepts in this book that you will learn to do the same.

Let's look at where we are at this moment. How do you feel? Are you happy with your map and your mission statement? Are you reading it daily and allowing it to be your guide? Does it serve to remind you of what you need to be aware of? Have you included a reminder to love yourself and treat yourself with the kindness you are deserving of?

If you feel ready, let's move up to the next step. If not, please go back and take more time. You are deserving of the time and effort it takes to move step by step. Stop now if you feel like you can't move past this point or at least pause and look for the beauty right where you are. If you truly cannot move on or push past the anger or hurt please seek professional help or speak to someone you trust. Finding someone who can help you move past the limited view of your past, enables you to move ahead. You must look for the answers that will allow you to continue this journey with me. You deserve real and lasting happiness free of your past conditions. By making the needed changes and learning to be kind to yourself, you will find that those words that hurt you in the past will wash away. The daily work we do will be like the water moving over a stone. It will shape you into something new and wonderful but the process does take time.

We now have a compass to set us in a new direction and we will not allow anything to set us off course. We will not be looking in that rear view mirror. Acknowledge within yourself that your memory of what was said to you could be limited by the small distorted view of that mirror. Looking back will not move us forward. You need no validation, and you can choose to make the decision to move on. It does not matter if anyone knows, believes or understands your past. You know it and you have been given a gift of choice. Choose to not let it be a shackle weighing you down; choose to move on. Visualize the river and remind yourself that to enjoy the trip you need to look at the beauty of the unlimited horizon ahead of you. So, spend no more time worrying about what others think. We still have much work to do!

Think about how far we have come. We have begun to quiet the noise others create by not allowing their destructive dialogue to affect you. That is all behind you now. We have created a map to guide our journey so we can begin creating ourselves in the light. Please do not sabotage yourself by successfully quieting the noise created by others but unable to move to the next step.

If you are ready, please step up with both feet resting firmly on the next step. Look down at where you started and acknowledge the progress we have made. Close your eyes and look around at the picture in your mind. The darkness at the bottom of the stairs is becoming darker as we move up towards the light. Can you now visualize the light within your spirit? It is important that you acknowledge any change you may feel. Are you thinking more clearly? Do you feel an inner calm? Are you able to notice more easily which noises to ignore? In your mind picture yourself standing on the stair strong and sure. Notice the subtle changes from within and acknowledge those changes so they can help to move you forward. When you feel ready let's move on.

We need to spend time looking at what we say to ourselves in our mind. The self-talk we come up with can be limiting and destructive. In this very important part of our enlightenment we will once again become aware, but this time it is what we are saying to ourselves. We all have become very adept at over thinking and over analyzing. We tend to repeat things that were hurtful to our spirit light again and again. By repeatedly acknowledging them we give them validation.

What we say to ourselves can be more damaging to our spirit than anything said by others. We tend to label ourselves with self-destructive words. We know ourselves well and when we allow ourselves free reign in our minds we know how to aim right at our weakest point.

It was so surprising when I started this part of the journey how often I caught myself being critical and negative of myself. I never would have spoken to anyone like I spoke to myself. Every time I caught myself saying something self-destructive, I would write down the negative thoughts. Page after page of my journal was overflowing with hurtful words directed at myself. In an attempt to change the reflex of immediate harm to my being, I created an affirmation card to carry in my purse. I would place it within my sight to serve as a constant reminder of the direction I was moving. I had not fully realized how much of a part the self-destructive thoughts played in who I was. Those words spoken in my mind were invisible shackles that kept me from becoming who I wanted to become.

This may be a hard concept for some to grasp since there are so many different ways to hurt yourself with words. I have included some of my realizations, which are just a few ways I caught myself allowing negativity and damaging talk to creep into my mind. See if you see yourself in any of these.

> I would tell myself what I wanted to achieve was impossible before I even tried it. I would come up with so many reasons it could not be done that I never allowed myself to start.

> I would begin my day and one small thing would go wrong. I would immediately convince myself that the entire day would be much the same. Everything that did not go "right" I would credit to the awful day I had pre-planned in my head.

> I would make a mistake on something small and go over and over it in my mind. I never re-directed my thoughts on how to avoid the mistake in the future. Rather, I focused on criticizing myself for making a mistake. I would replay it in my mind it until it had a life of its own.

I would hear troublesome news or a problem would arise and I immediately created a worst-case scenario. I would envision an awful ending and spend time being upset, when I had no idea of what the outcome would be and no control over the circumstances.

I would continue to complain in my mind about something small and insignificant that could have been easily resolved. Somehow in my mind it was more comforting to remain in that state than step back and find a solution.

What was the common theme among all these scenarios? Everything that occurred happened in my head. I could have made different choices and avoided the damage I allowed it to take on my spirit. But until I became aware I did little to recognize the harm I was causing myself.

It is time again to pull out your journal and think back to the steps that will again help you prepare. Find a quiet spot to sit and draw the calmness to your heart. Listen for the whispering voice telling you what your heart is saying. Write the following question at the top of a new page

Am I aware of what I am saying to myself?

Say It To Yourself

Spend a few days aware of the dialog in your head. Keep your tablet with you for the next few days. Write down your thoughts. Become aware of what you are saying to yourself. Write negative and positive self-talk. In addition, look closely for your responses when someone says something you don't like or agree with. You should be getting more adept at quieting the noise of others but this is a great test of the earlier work we did.

What was your response when you chose not to allow their darkness in? Did you still respond with a negative thought? If so, you still need to work on editing what to let in and how you will react to it. Even if you didn't let the words affect you, your reaction may suggest that more work is needed. Be aware that you need to be vigilant on filtering the noise from others and what you are saying to yourself in each situation. Are you overly critical of yourself? What adjectives have you used? All of these need to be looked at and addressed. After a few days of taking notes sit down and review each page.

> Does what you are saying to yourself reflect what you really think of yourself?
>
> How is it affecting your mood and ultimately your life?

What might happen if you changed how you spoke to yourself?

Would it have an impact on how you would expect to be treated by others?

What do you need to do to make a lasting change to the way you speak to yourself?

I will share a few observations I had when viewing my own notes. These realizations helped change the way I was thinking. I hope you will read them and take them to heart as we continue the journey.

Where did I come up with the notion that I needed to be perfect? Why do I think I need to be the best at something in order to be worthy of any form of self-appreciation? I never demanded perfection from others why would I demand it of myself?

Why did I allow a worry or problem to escalate in my mind? If there was nothing I could do to alter the outcome then creating a worse-case scenario served no purpose. It took me a very long time to work through the fact that my worrying about something did not affect the outcome.

How can I move past a legitimate complaint in my mind? The answer was not to ignore the complaint but to turn it around into a question. Complaining does nothing to solve the problem at hand. Changing a complaint to a question allows you to look at the horizon and not in the rear view mirror. I found by switching the complaint to a question I tricked my mind into asking for a solution.

Look at how it works.

Complaint: I never have any time for myself. You are just stating a fact, nothing changes.

Acknowledgement: Yes it is hard to find time when there is always so much to do. This does nothing but set it more firmly in your mind by reinforcing the fact that you have no time for yourself. Still nothing has changed.

Turn it into a question: How can I find more time for myself? Look at what immediately begins to happen. Your mind begins to formulate thoughts on possible solutions.

Complaint: You never help me clean the house!

Acknowledgement: You are right I don't do much around here!

Question: How can we work together to get the house clean?

Complaint: We will never be able to finish the project on time.

Acknowledgement: You are right we will never finish with all that still needs to be done.

Question: What do we need to do to make sure this project is completed on time?

It works every time! Changing the complaint into a question energizes you for action and stimulates your imagination to search for a solution.

This one little switch in my mind has brought resolution to so many areas in my life. Please feel free to use it every time you hear a complaint, even if the complaint is from you!

The previous section we looked at addressed the negative self-talk within our own minds. Take a few moments and look at the positive self-talk you wrote down. How much, if any, of the conversation with your self was encouraging and uplifting? Did you notice a difference in the ratio of negative to positive talk? If you did not have much negative self-talk that is wonderful. You already have a foothold on the slippery slope of self-negativity. If you had a lot of negative self-talk, do not to worry. This is an area where reflecting on the problem can change the outcome.

Practice being more aware of what you are thinking about all the time. You can actually improve your self-esteem rather quickly with a switch in how you treat yourself within your mind.

However, looking for what is missing from our positive self-talk can be a bit trickier because it is not present; we need to go searching specifically for each quality that needs to be present. Gratitude, happiness, love, faith, acceptance, passion and purpose need to be part of your mind's vocabulary to find your *everything*. We will address these in the upcoming chapters. You already have enough to work on now with improving your positive self-talk and diminishing, and even eliminating, your negative self-talk.

One powerful piece that may be missing from your self-talk, but important to acknowledge now, is hope. I realized early in my journey that hope was missing in my self-talk. After a long period of attempting to add hope I realized that hope is not just a piece of the puzzle, but rather the glue that holds the puzzle together.

Hope is expectation, optimism, faith, and possibility. Hope is the belief that you can put the puzzle together and keep it held together strong and complete. Hope is the intention before the action to make it happen. Hope is one of the motivating factors in searching for the light that brightens your spirit. You need to have hope as your companion as you move forward with me on this journey.

Now is time for you to create your occupant rules and your affirmation card. Let's start with your occupant rules. I call them occupant rules because if you had someone occupying your living space you would certainly create rules. And so it should be the same for your mind. Take out your journal and look again at the negative self-talk you have written over the past few days. Review it and see if you can define areas of internal dialog that are obvious. Look for reoccurring themes. Some of the most common are low self- esteem, self-doubt, self-criticism, focused self-anger, blame, rationalization, denial, competition, jealousy, anger and perfection.

These are to be avoided as they are destructive and will not lead you in the direction of peace and contentment. They will only serve to dim the light we have started to brighten. We need to focus on removing these from our mind. Again our best tool is awareness. Write out some occupant rules for yourself. Include positive declarations in the sentence and make sure you write in the present tense. I have listed a few examples of your occupant rules below to give you an idea of what we are looking for.

Within me I have all I need to change the negative self-talk that I have left unchecked for too long.

I will no longer allow myself to feel guilt for making a mistake. I will work to rationally keep the mistake in perspective and not allow it to occupy space in my mind. I will allow it to remain for a few minutes while I work to make the corrections. I will then release it and never allow it to return to my thoughts.

I will not allow myself to be disrespected and treated poorly. I now realize that in order to love someone else, I first need to love myself. I will learn to love myself and set standards for my care. Then and only then can I be at a place in my life that I can acknowledge the beauty that resides within me.

Now write out your rules for the occupant in your mind. Review these daily to remind yourself of your vulnerable areas. Add additional rules as you become aware of areas that need attention.

Now write your affirmation note to remind yourself you are worthy!

It should be short and sweet. Write it as if you are speaking gently and softly to yourself. Make it a love note to your spirit.

It may say something like -

By being true to who I am becoming, has enabled me to brighten the light in my spirit and allowed me to recognize the wondrous gift that I am.

I stand with arms wide open accepting that I am a gift to myself and I deserve love and happiness. I am now a stranger to the darkness as light fills my spirit.

I see now that I am created to be a reflection of the love and kindness of my maker. And I will be eternally grateful that the light within my spirit did not extinguish but remained lit waiting for me to discover its beauty and power.

When you are satisfied with what it says rewrite it on a note card or small piece of cardboard. Laminate it so it remains intact through its many travels. Keep it with you at all times to remind yourself that you are worthy of love and kindness from everyone including yourself.

Now I want you to look within and acknowledge something wonderful about yourself. It needs to be positive and it must be about you. It cannot involve or be about anyone else. We are working on strengthening our spirit by acknowledging our goodness and reinforcing the foundation we are building upon. Remember we cannot truly love another completely until we love ourselves completely; and we cannot love ourselves until we acknowledge the best part of us.

I have spent enormous amounts of energy living up to what people believed me to be. I never wanted to let anyone down by not being who they thought I was. Not being your authentic self and living up to others expectations is exhausting and takes a huge toll on your entire being. When you are in this state you will never find the energy or courage to make yourself the focus, and ultimately find your genuine self. Becoming who you really are, and knowing how to keep your spirit bright, takes little effort once you acknowledge that the internal changes you made are moving you in the direction you need to go.

At this point, I hope you are willing to look into the darkness and see the light brightening. And we are well on our way now to finding the secret place that lies within you.

Start a new page and write the following on the top line:

I am a wondrous gift and I love myself. I acknowledge the goodness within me. I am _____.

I must admit to you that I shed many tears over this sentence. I had never said anything like this to myself. What a tragedy it was to have lived a life so long without acknowledging that I was a gift from a power greater than myself.

Fill in the space with a word you ask your spirit to provide. Quiet your mind and ask your heart to bring the word to you. It may take some time for you to receive it. You will know when the right word is brought forth because it will feel right when you say it. It will tickle your soul. If your ego has delivered the word to you ignore it and keep asking.

You will recognize your ego's word because it will be critical and dark. It may take time for your dark noisy side or your ego to give in to the quiet, peaceful side we are working to nurture. Keep asking and the word will come to you. After you receive the word, fill in the blank. Read it again, believe it, feel it in your heart. Close your eyes and know that you are what you have written. What you are reading is true, you truly are that wonderful word. And your faith in believing it will allow you to rise to be the most amazing part of who you are becoming. Tell yourself everyday you are something wonderful and miraculous. As we travel further into the journey you will be able to add more words to the first word on your list. Go back to this page and reread the sentence daily adding words as they come to you, and you feel they match to who you are becoming.

We can now move to the next step while still being aware of everything we have learned to this point. The hardest work is done. The steps now become smaller and the work moves to one of more awareness, realization and enlightenment. Can you see who you are becoming? Are you beginning to see that you are the light and that you alone will be the solution to brightening your spirit?

Let us continue our journey together armed with our occupant rules, affirmation card and awareness of how our ego will repeatedly try to undermine our attempts to become who we want to be.

Your Beautiful Spirit

"People are like stained-glass windows. They sparkle and shine when the sun is out, but when the darkness sets in their true beauty is revealed only if there is light from within".

Elisabeth Kübler-Ross

What is this spirit that we are so interested in brightening? The dictionary gives its description as *the vital force that characterizes a human being as being alive.*

Before looking more deeply at our spirit let's look at where we are in our journey. Close your eyes and see yourself. Are you ready to move to the next stair? Are you working daily to quiet all the noise from yourself and from others? Is your map inspiring you when you read it daily? Are you sitting quietly for a few moments each day and finding the calm within and are you aware of more clarity within your being? Look down at the darkness where we came from. You can barely see where you began. Can you see the light at the top is becoming brighter as we approach? Are you able to look to the horizon ahead? Then you are ready to move on.

Prior to my enlightenment I would have told you that the spirit is the source of who we were meant to be. Our spirit is the center of our being from which the essence of our being originates. Our spirit having been destined by the grace of our higher power or maybe it was luck or fate whose life was blessed and whose life had encountered a more difficult path. Those who were blessed remained untested by difficult challenges allowing their spirit to more easily remain bright. Then there are the unlucky people who seem to be burdened with profound challenges those of great sadness, desperation and loss. Challenges we are not sure we would survive.

Much like our soul, I didn't think much about my spirit being a part of me that I needed to nurture much less become aware of its brightness. I knew it was there and believed if I was a good person and believed in a higher power, then my level of happiness and peace would be in direct relation to the number of challenges I would be given over my lifetime. Someone who has had much sadness or tragedy in their life would have a dim spirit light. They have been given the destiny of a long and challenging journey. It made no sense to me that someone who had a difficult journey could still be happy and bright of spirit. I also believed that as we age the light in our spirit dims a result of the time eroding its brightness.

I also believed that there were those people who had very dark spirits, the people who did not keep sacred the right and wrong rules established in my mind. Of course these were the wrong doers, the breakers of the most sacred rules, the murderers and criminals.

It was during my trip through the mountains when I realized the answer I was searching for was always within me. I was forever looking outside of myself waiting for things to be "right" before I could be happy. I was living a life of setting up expectations for myself and others, only to end up disappointed. Until the day of my enlightenment, when my journey truly began, did I begin to look at every possible remedy. It was then that I realized that one simple word held the answer.

Spirit.

Connecting the puzzle pieces would involve more than just my spirit but everything I needed to complete the puzzle was held safe there.

What do I know now about our Spirit? I know it is the most wondrous and mysterious part of our essence. Hidden and protected from our ego's naturally destructive ways, its light dims but never is completely dark. It is the foundation of vast and unending peace and love and the source of our true happiness. It holds safe our inner peace and even when the seas appear rough on the surface, our spirit is the calm that lies below. It is always peaceful and loving and is never judgmental. It holds unlimited love, acceptance and forgiveness. It is the safe place within you can always return to once you honor its existence and comprehend its importance to *your everything*. It is also the place we can look to find our true self.

Discovering the depth and brightness of our spirit, we can then be, true to who we are to be. Gradually it becomes less important who others see us as, and more important who we become for ourselves. The goal is to become a loving and joyful person possessing a bottomless well of peace in their heart the depth of which cannot be measured. It is then we can become ourselves and are the calm under the rough surface of the sea.

However, since our spirit is very quiet and peaceful it is often harder to hear than the loud feelings of the ego that easily overtake it. Looking for the ego at work will alert you to the danger it holds for your well being. Traits like anger, jealousy, fear, blame, rationalization and hurt, if allowed, will attempt to silence our spirit by creating such noise within that you can no longer hear or feel its existence. The ego is quite adept at creating excitement and amusement, tricking you into believing it is benefiting you. The ego is delighted and amused by the turmoil it creates.

While the calm and peaceful spirit can seem quite boring and predictable, it is within its depth that real and lasting purpose and passion emerges. The excitement the ego bestows upon you must be constantly replenished to remain in that state. It is within this never- ending quest to sustain the feeling of excitement the ego brings that leads you towards the darkness. Conversely, the spirit's purpose and passion is one of motivation that keeps you progressing and creates its own momentum in its quest to uncover your authentic self and true happiness.

Let's look at our ego and its devastating effect on the brightness of our spirit. Ego is the darkness within our spirit. It is under that cover of darkness that the ego does its best work. It is the helper of the uncertain. If you do not know who you are, or have an idea of who want to become, the ego will create someone for you to be. The ego will act, very quickly to create noise and drown out the quiet spiritual side that struggles to be heard. It claims to protect you from harm but really darkens the light allowing little view of your choices. It eclipses even the dimmest light in your spirit thus making the search for who you want to be harder to envision. We can never rid ourselves of our ego but once we brighten and strengthen our spirit, we can then easily recognize it and be aware to quiet its voice.

The more you move towards the light, you will learn to recognize its many harmful traits and deceiving qualities. For now I will help you become aware of the many ways the ego will attempt to limit the brightness within.

Reasoning – the ego removes looking honestly at what occurred and moves right to reasoning the event away. It rationalizes something you know in your heart is not true to your being. It allows you to defer remorse or guilt for something hurtful you have done or said to another by justifying it. In your mind you had a "good" reason for what you have done.

Blame - the ego removes you completely from the equation and blames its darkness solely upon another person or on uncontrollable circumstances.

Competition - the ego receives its validation by constantly comparing itself with others. It is the killer of any form of contentment and peace. It is never satisfied always wanting more. The ego is on a constant search to place a rank on your worth not based on who you are but rather how you compare to others. If we have more or better then we can feel superior to others. If we have less then jealousy enters to feed the empty spot in our ego.

Conditions - The ego needs to be constantly replenished and conditions are one way to assure that it continues being nourished. For example,

I will be happy when…

I will feel gratitude when…

I will feel love when….

The ego is never satisfied and it will keep you waiting for conditions to be perfect before it allows the light to enter your spirit. True to the ego's dark nature and its constant quest for more, a constant stream of conditions will be supplied as you continue to strive for what will be enough. But if allowed to flourish, your ego will always keep the realization of true happiness just beyond your reach.

Arrogance – One of our ego's tricks can be seen as we move to love ourselves without conditions. Not keeping the ego in check while learning to love who you are becoming, is another of the ego's favorite indulgences. You can certainly love yourself, speak to yourself gently and demand respect for yourself without thinking that you are superior. If we refuse the temptation to compare ourselves to others then you avoid creating a label of self-importance in your mind. The end result is truly about loving yourself and appreciating the amazing qualities you possess and not about comparing those qualities to those of others.

Fear- The ego loves fear because nothing will stop your progress and darken your light as quickly as fear will. If we do not know who we are, fear will be happy to oblige and fill in the space with doubt, anger, defensiveness, jealousy and self-pity. Fear will rob you of any hope you have of breaking through the darkness and finding *your everything*. If we have the courage to look, really look at what we fear and make a conscious choice and decide if it is a real or perceived threat, we can then move past it.

One area that we must address when speaking of the ego are the limitation we place on our mind when we create labels. Each label we create is the ego's way of limiting our view ahead. The more labels we create the more set the picture attached to that label is ingrained in us. By not looking deeper than the label you created, it becomes easier to justify and rationalize that label. The end result is that the ego wins and you lose by the effect it has upon your spirit. It is very hard to change a label once it is established in our mind. So I found the best way to get past it was by not allowing myself to label anything.

What exactly do I mean by label? Labels take many forms. I view it as any descriptive word that attaches a preconceived belief or opinion to someone or something as being a label. I will list a few and see if a picture or feeling pops in your head: pretty, handsome, ugly, rich, poor, overweight and skinny. Those are just a few of the visual labels but the list is endless.

Picture in your mind someone you don't know coming towards you from a distance. Would any of those labels pop into your head? Of course, and there will be a judgment attached to the label you placed. Could your label be your preconceived belief and be completely inaccurate or wrong? Could the label you place be limited or affected by your life experiences? Does the label you attached allow you to rank yourself and your value above or below them? Does your judgment make it more or less likely you will engage them in any way? How much are you limiting yourself by attaching a label?

Would it better serve you to avoid labels and keep your mind open to any possibility? This is an example of another way in which self-talk is limiting our light. Although not directed at ourselves this time, it does harm to our spirit in addition to restricting our mind's opportunities to grow. Prior to becoming enlightened I would label everyone. All people who I came in contact with were put in a category and stayed there until they proved their way out of it. I even labeled myself. Once I understood that it was a label and did not define who I was, I gave myself permission to be true to myself. Once my spirit became bright I realized labeling severely limited my ability to look beyond the label. Dismissing it from my life freed me to become less judgmental and more compassionate. Forgiving faults and mistakes was much easier with compassion and love in my heart instead of having a dark spirit filled with comparisons and competition.

There is a great need on this journey to quiet our ego and contemplate peace and calmness within our spirit. The best way to embrace the comfort of calmness within your spirit is by being consciously calm. Meditation, prayer or just quiet contemplation brings us closer to the realization of the importance of our spirit and higher power. It is the place within us that is as close to what we imagine who we were created to be. It is during this quiet time that the realizations we are working towards will switch from confusing and complex, to simple thoughts that have great clarity. You will begin to see how all the pieces of the puzzle fit together to make you complete.

Our awareness this time will be on keeping the ego in check. Do not let it pull you into the darkness of your spirit. Make it show itself in your light so that you can access it.

For the next few days please be aware of the ways your ego is trying to draw you into the darkness. You may notice that the calmness you have created within has already begun to keep you in the light and the darkness feels uncomfortable. You may occasionally be duped by the ego's tricks. Remember we are being transformed and it is a process to become our brightest. What is important is your awareness, and with that awareness comes a conscious choice. The more you choose moving towards the light the more you move away from the darkness.

So take your journal out and write the following questions.

How is my ego drawing me away from who I want to become? Am I limiting myself by creating labels?

Have your journal as your companion for the next few days. Write down situations you know were brought forth from your ego. When you feel that your ego has grasped you, access the situation. Determine where you were and who you were with. Did you allow yourself to be drawn in or did you stop yourself when you realized your ego and not your spirit was engaged? Did it serve you well to remember who we are becoming and the direction we are headed? Did you trade a few moments of excitement giving in to the ego's quest for power? Can you look back and see how it dims your brightness when you contemplate its effect upon you?

Write an affirmation for the each situation you have recorded in your journal. Think of how you might look at it from the spirit's perspective next opportunity. You may end up with pages or just a few examples. Sometimes it is hard to define when the ego is at work. Just look for all the traits I spoke of earlier. We inherently know in our heart and spirit which side, the dark or the light, is speaking to us. Trust yourself. You have worked hard on the growth and development of your spirit and on growing the wonderful part of you that was once hidden. This is another awareness we need to take with us on our beautiful journey.

Let's move on knowing the danger of allowing our ego to choose our perspective instead of our bright spirit.

Choices

"The greatest power a person possesses is the power to choose".

J Martin Kohe

Every day we are alive we have this amazing ability to make choices. Some choices are easy to make and some are difficult. Some we make fully aware of all our options and some we feel we have no choice at all, though we usually do. Some require discipline to make the right choice and some require no discipline. Some choices are made from emotion and some from our more logical side. Some are the result of a world seen as black or white and right or wrong.

Some of the choices we make are made without looking at all the choices we actually have. This leaves us with not being aware of all the choices and options we have available.

There are even levels of choice. Choosing what to wear, buy or eat are choices we make quite often. These are usually pretty easy choices since the risk and

Choices

consequences for making the wrong choice is small. Choosing your profession, job, house or even a spouse are much more important. But these choices still leave you with an option to change the situation if you have made the wrong choice. Not making a choice is sometimes an option but it is still a choice.

If you look at our journey so far you will realize you have made some pretty important choices during this process. The choices you have made I hope were the result of looking with your spirit's light and not at the darkness. You may not have realized just how many choices you have made. You chose this book, and made the choice to work step by step to become aware and change the course of your journey. Do you realize how your choices are changing your essence? Have you made different choices looking at things with an enlightened spirit? Are you reading your mission statement to remind yourself daily who you are becoming? Can you see yourself further up the steps, further from the darkness where you were with your face now turned to the brightness above? Are you able to add words to your list acknowledging to yourself the wondrous gift that you are? Can you visualize the light within your spirit and realize that this is the sum of all your choices so far?

This next step on our journey requires you not to simply realize that you make choices but to be aware of the choices you are making. You will learn to consider your choices and decide if the choices will move you in the direction of *your everything*.

Let's look at some of the ways our choices can enrich our lives and strengthen who we are becoming.

Choosing to look at and treat everyone as an equal. For me, this choice became easier the brighter my spirit became and the more I grew to love myself. I simply grew to believe, that anyone under the beautiful sky that joins us all into one, is my equal. There is no one better or worse than me. I do not feel within my heart compelled to compare myself with anyone. I do believe that we all have been created for a purpose. Though we all have different circumstances, those circumstances do not define your value as a person. It is a life changing transformation to not see yourself in comparison, but in unity with another. The ability to stop labeling or ranking others, as well as yourself, frees your mind to think more about the whole of the world and less about yourself. Yes, this journey is about you and your spirit but not about your ego's needs and wants. To have a heart filled with love for everyone without restrictions is a result of your choice to love all without limitations.

Choices

Choosing to look with gratitude. I can choose to look at all I have and say with a grateful heart - thank you! However, I can still possess a great appreciation for things that I may receive in the future. Most importantly, I know that I already have the most important possessions I will ever receive already within me. Or I can choose to look at all I have and say it is not enough and set about spending the remainder of my journey searching for what will be enough. It is a choice.

Choosing to live with grace and gentleness. I can choose to live my life possessing qualities of grace and gentleness. I can look upon others with understanding and kindness treating every person with dignity. I can choose to look at each individual believing there is goodness within them and help them on their search for their gifts. Moving forward on my journey I will quietly seek to accept what I cannot change but never failing to try.

Choosing who will accompany you on this journey. When we began I asked you to be wary of the effect that people with a dark spirit and the light stealers have on you. You were cautioned to make sure that they did not pull you into their darkness. Now that we have advanced further on our journey, we will try to understand who they are and the choices that are now yours to make. Dark of Spirit people are those who will have none of your happiness. They are so entrenched in their ways that your light filled spirit actually bothers them to the point of you being an annoyance. They will verbally attempt to create a great wind to extinguish your newfound light. This is where your newly acquired skill of awareness will be of great use. Being aware and understanding what they are trying to do will allow you to reject their attempt to have you join them in their darkness. Look for the traits we spoke of earlier such as jealousy, anger, blame and denial.

Light stealers are an entirely different challenge. They are much more devious about darkening your spirit. They will be very covert about their need to steal your energy and light. They are persistent in drawing you into a confrontation, or a negative or angry verbal exchange. Agreeing, rationalizing or joining in with them only feeds their ego, and supplies energy to their dark spirit while dimming your own light. Defending your position, disagreeing or engaging in any form with a light stealer is a useless endeavor. The only answer is to steadfastly refuse to engage. The stronger and clearer your light, the easier it will be to achieve. If you do not supply the fuel to replenish their ego they will simply retreat but usually not without first leveling one last verbal attack. Being fully aware of their intent and determined to remain true to yourself you can now choose to simply ignore their hurtful words and move on leaving them within their darkness.

Choices

Choosing to be responsible for making my own light bright. I do not look for others to fill my spirit by expecting them to be who or what I need them to be. This creates unrealistic expectations resulting in harm to both spirits. I will be true to my own light and allow those close to me to create for themselves the light to fill their own spirit.

Choosing to keep filling my spirit with the light every day by awareness and appreciation of all my free gifts. Are you making time daily to review your map, and adding to your list of inspirational words, that describe who you are becoming? Did you seek and find beauty and happiness today within and around you? These need to become habits for you. Replace your old habits that did not serve you with good habits to move you towards the light.

Choosing to not allow conditions to determine the happiness I allow in my life. I will learn to dance during any storm that may occur in my life. I will refuse to keep waiting for the storm to pass to enjoy my life.

Now let's look for some choices you will be making over the next few days. Bring your journal out and think back to the steps that will again help you prepare for your writing. Find a quiet spot to sit and draw the calmness to your heart. Listen for the whispering voice telling you what your heart is saying. Write down a few choices you needed to make that day. Be aware of the options you have and if the choices you made are true to who you are becoming and who you want to be. Are you allowing the ever brightening light within your spirit to be your guide? Is your ego in check and not affecting your choices? You should feel great gratitude for the awareness of your choices.

After you have spent a few days writing down some of the choices you have made, look deep within those choices to recognize the spirit's light guiding the choices you have made. If you do not feel you were successful in allowing your spirit to guide you keep working at it. Continue writing each day until you see the light and not the darkness guiding your choices.

Please look back at your map and your mission statement and see if you can incorporate into your map some of the knowledge you have gained while looking at your choices.

Do you realize that the choices you are making are really the oars for your boat? Those oars, your choices, allow you at any point to slow down and linger in the beauty of your life. Or, by choice alter the direction in which you are headed, if it is not serving your spirit light.

Choices

Let's choose to continue on our journey remembering to keep our ego in check and making our choices in the brightness of the light within our spirit.

Gratitude

"Gratitude unlocks the fullness of life. It turns what we have into enough, and more. It turns denial into acceptance, chaos into order confusion to clarity. It can turn a meal into a feast, house into a home, a stranger into a friend. Gratitude makes sense of our past, brings peace for today, and creates a better vision for tomorrow"
Melody Beattie

We have suffered a great loss in our lives when we lose the ability to look at everything with a grateful heart. We have been given this amazing life and every single day no matter the circumstances, we should give thanks. If we have done our work to this point you should be seeing everything with more clarity and appreciation.

Let's take a look with gratitude at our journey so far. You are still climbing each stair and moving closer to the light. By being aware, you have been successful at quieting the internal and external noise, and can now hear when your heart speaks. You are well on your way to defining *your everything*. You are realizing that you are a gift to yourself and you are treating yourself with the kindness and self-love that is freeing your spirit and allowing it to soar. We know what to look for when our ego speaks instead of our spirit. We are also able to recognize the limitations in others so that compassion, not anger, is our response. The words love, peace and happiness have more meaning for you now because you can feel them and not just say them.

What does being grateful mean to our journey? Gratitude is one of our choices. It is the ability to look at things with awareness and realization and understand there is more than one view or perspective. You can choose to view things with an ungrateful heart believing that what you have is not enough, or look with gratitude and believe that you already have *your everything*. Whichever way you choose to believe you will be right. Your spirit cannot become bright and strong without gratitude and appreciation. You cannot be truly happy without gratitude. True happiness, without conditions, comes from gratitude for all you have. You cannot love yourself completely without gratitude for the gift of your essence.

There are so many benefits of living a life of gratitude beyond the ones reflected in our happiness. People that adopt gratitude as a lasting change have a distinct health advantage over the not-so-grateful people. We all understand the link between stress and disease. Gratitude can help us better manage stress and worry and give us the ability to cope with everyday problems.

So to enrich our life we need to make gratitude a part of our awareness. Every day we are surrounded by examples to appreciate all we have been given. Every person knows of, or has read about, people with challenges far greater than ours, yet they remain grateful. Let's not wait to be sick to appreciate our health. Let's not forget to tell someone how much they mean to us before they are no longer with us. Let's choose to be joyful every day before this part of our journey ends. Gratitude makes everyday a day for you to celebrate.

So how do you continue to be motivated to improve yourself and your life, if you are satisfied with what you have? First, satisfaction and gratitude are completely different. Satisfaction is to be content with the way things are and does not give much motivation for change. Gratitude is simply being thankful. Being thankful does not affect your ability to strive for more. Looking for more, and being grateful for what you have, is a balance. There is a secret to achieving that balance within your life.

You can strive to want more from your life while still remaining eternally grateful for what you have, if the motivating factors are passion or purpose. If you are blessed to have found a passion in your life, you understand that it propels and motivates you. It would never allow you to be stagnant. The motion it creates in your life is a wave that will carry you to the end of your journey. But passion is not independent of gratitude. Passion's motives are pure. They are a result of a given grace and originate from the deepest part of your being, your spirit. People do not usually harm others or themselves over the pursuit of their passion unless ego casts its darkness over it.

Purpose is the other quality that allows you to want more and still remain grateful for all your gifts. If you have a purpose driving your motivation and that motivation is focused upon learning and growing, it is easier to create the balance. Sometimes the purpose is simply to improve or enhance yourself, share your gifts, change a bad situation, or help others. Anytime your purpose is one of bettering your situation, or the situation of another, it is easier to balance gratitude and ambition. It is when darkness is the motivating force behind purpose that it becomes difficult. Look for labels and comparisons to expose the purpose and the darkness.

Let's take out our journal. I hope it is filled to the brim with notes from your journey so far. We will now work on becoming aware of gratitude and its affect upon you and your spirit. Remember, much like awareness, this will become a habit. It will take work to make gratitude an essential part of your daily existence. Gratitude will need to be a constant to guide you on your journey. Practicing gratitude will be enjoyable because you are learning to brighten your spirit. With each new opportunity to apply gratitude you will see and feel immediate results.

Take your journal out and write Day One at the top of the page. Create a separate page for each day up to day seven. On the page for Day One, write one star (*) on the top line. Add one star per day (*) so Day Two would have two stars. Continue this for seven days so at the end you have a piece of paper with Day Seven and seven stars written on it. Starting today, Day One write down something you are grateful for. Make it something that you are able to reframe with gratitude and optimism. Choose things that you normally would have viewed negatively. Or, they could be things that you have just become grateful for because now you are aware of their presence. When you have finished the first week, look back at all that you were grateful for.

Can you see the benefit to your spirit in changing your thinking? Continue for the next two weeks finding at least seven things to be grateful for each day. You may find that some days you have many things to be grateful for and there may be days you find the assignment difficult. Most of us have not trained our mind to listen to our heart. Our heart whispers and tells us to look at things with grateful eyes. We must retrain our mind to think in this new and exciting way. Three weeks is the period in which the mind begins to accept something new as a habit. Three weeks later you will have been grateful for one hundred and twenty six new things. Your bright spirit will be the reward to looking with grateful eyes at the very things you took for granted in the past.

One area that we must not overlook is gratefulness for people closest to us. Often times it is the people that are nearest to us that we appreciate the least. If we neglect to purposefully look with love, gratitude and appreciation for their best qualities, it will become a habit to notice all of their worst qualities. We need to develop a habit to include people, not just situations, when growing in gratitude. Acknowledging the good qualities in someone, after seeing only the bad qualities, may be difficult.

Situations may arise that offer an opportunity to look with gratitude at those close to you. However, your ego may be impeding your ability to look at people close to you in that new light. You may have been hurt or treated badly or you may feel they are dark of spirit. Maybe you feel that you are giving in if you acknowledge any good within them. It is much more fun for your ego to hold on to your old way of thinking.

Forgiveness of others is a gift you give to yourself, not to others. Listen to your spirit's quiet and peaceful side. It takes time and much effort to change the view. It is much more fun for your ego to stir up trouble and make you believe that it is serving you by ignoring the good in people you need to forgive.

We will only find the good in everyone when we look for and acknowledge it. By verbally recognizing the good we see, we let them know that we are grateful for that goodness. They will then begin to feel the light within themselves brighten and may choose to nurture that brightness. This process works for everyone including children. However, if you search deep and listen to your heart's whispers, and still cannot find any qualities worthy of acknowledging within them, and can find no gratitude for them in your life, you will need to make a choice.

You will need to rethink the part these people play in your life. There are people who are so dark of spirit that they will engulf you in their darkness. They will not allow you to see even the smallest glimmer of light within them. In the Choices chapter we looked at the dark of spirit and the light stealers. You are stronger now and more aware.

You have the right to choose how much they will be allowed to interact with you. You must consider the positive effect removing them from your life will have on your spirit. You have the right to disconnect from anyone whom you know deep within your heart to be harmful to you and your spirit.

When practicing your newfound gratitude be cautious and remember we are but a pebble. Not everyone will be grateful for all things or appreciate what you do for them. Expecting people to embrace gratitude as you have, will only set you up for unfulfilled expectations. The result will be unhappiness and a dimming of your spirit. If you want others to be grateful, then you must be grateful yourself. It is a cultivated trait and the more your share it, the more it expands and spreads. Others, including our children, will pick up on gratitude rather quickly if we make it our constant companion.

Let's commit everyday to look with grateful eyes at all that is around and within us. Soon it will require no effort at all and become one with the light in your spirit.

Let us now take another step towards the light and look for our happiness.

Happiness

"People spend a lifetime searching for happiness; looking for peace. They chase idle dreams, addictions, religions, even other people, hoping to fill the emptiness that plagues them. The irony is the only place they ever needed to search was within".

Ramona L. Anderson

We have come a long way. Can you see more clearly that this journey is about you? Is it now easier to see that to become who you want to be, you need to accept that your happiness can be found by you and you alone. Your true happiness lies within the brightness of your spirit and the whispers of your heart. Your spirit is not dependent upon conditions to be perfect for it to be illuminated. The realization that your spirit is present with you every moment of everyday allows you to embrace and nurture its brightness. We cannot buy or own happiness; it is a free gift that is reflected by the brightness of your spirit. It lies in abundance within us but only if you know where to look; and only if you make the choice to reveal its presence. You take nothing away from another person by being happy yourself. In fact to the contrary, you free them to feel it radiating from within you and share in its light. There is an unlimited supply of light that lies within each of us.

Close your eyes and feel the warmth from the light we are moving ever closer to. The place at which we began is merely a memory. The steps are getting easier to climb now and with each step we feel that who we are becoming is more true to who we want to be. You should feel at ease knowing that as you become more and more aware of the choices you are making you are moving closer to who you want to become. Look everyday for the beauty that resides within and around you. Be grateful for the gift of awareness that changed how you look at your journey. Continue with me to moving ever closer to *your everything*.

It was at this point in my own journey that I found myself impatient for happiness to return. I would try to will it to appear. I would pretend to be happy. That brought back feelings of who I had been before I had started my journey. I was not going to allow myself to return there. I had come so far to feel joy and happiness. I was becoming who I wanted to become. I had learned to accept what I could not change and quiet the noise. I had looked into my heart and listened for the whispers within my heart. I could feel my spirit bright and strong and could see the beauty all around me. Why was happiness not magically appearing in my spirit? Had I been wrong? Had I done all the work to achieve happiness just to have the last piece of the puzzle be one that I would never find? Maybe there was still too much darkness for me to see it or maybe my spirit had been dark too long.

As I continued searching, I happened upon an article by Ekhart Tolle that read "you do not become good by trying to be good but by finding the goodness within you and allowing that goodness to emerge". I suddenly realized that I would find happiness again not by sheer will but by acknowledging it within me. I could allow my happiness to emerge, by changing my demand for its return to a peaceful request. By changing my mind's voice, and asking for guidance to reclaim it in a softer and gentler tone. By gradually changing these things true happiness was at last returned to me. My happiness was a priceless gift whose value is beyond measure.

But there were many lessons to be learned before I could ask for the happiness I was seeking. First and foremost, I needed to learn to live without putting conditions upon everything. I had to make certain that the result I wanted was equal to or exceeded, the condition I placed upon it before happiness could be present. What do I mean by that last statement? We all tend to delay happiness for no real reason. It is almost as if we are afraid of embracing happiness for fear of losing it. I know that at some time each of us has placed conditions on our happiness. For example, I will be happy when: I get married, I get a promotion, I have a baby, I lose weight and the list goes on. But even after we get the results we wanted and we *should* be happy, we instantly replace it with a new condition - forever keeping happiness just out of our reach.

This limiting behavior is much like always wanting more possessions the ego is always looking for something we do not have. When we climb into the boat we have this picture in our mind of what our lives will be like. Each picture may be slightly different but most involve finding Prince Charming or Cinderella, buying a beautiful castle and living together happily ever after. Even though we give no thought to the reality of life, we expect our lives to be filled with nothing but joy and happiness.

We decide how our life is going to be and place unrealistic conditions on everything and everyone. When you set unrealistic expectations for a condition of happiness and things don't turn out, disappointment is the outcome. Someone has let you down. We didn't get what we planned for, wanted, desired or expected. The question for you to think about is: How willing are you to let the disappointment affect you? We all face disappointments in our life but are you content to allow it to draw you into the darkness and permit it to affect your happiness?

We need to abandon the notion that when everything is exactly as we want it, then and only then, can we be happy. How many days, months and years are you willing to surrender waiting for things to be perfect for you to be happy? There are many circumstances that affect our life but we cannot allow them to define our life. If we know that things can, and will go wrong, why do we allow ourselves to expect perfect conditions before allowing happiness? We cannot delay happiness until your life matches the picture you have created in your mind.

One way to work through placing conditions, if you feel compelled to do so, is by making the condition something easily attainable. For example, I will be happy today… if I am alive, can get out of bed, if I have food to eat, or if I can see the blue sky. Then hold yourself to it. Allow the gift of happiness to return because you have met the condition. You will then become aware that you control your level of happiness and that you are also responsible for the conditions of your unhappiness.

There will be times in all our lives that devastating events happen causing real unhappiness. Death of a loved one, catastrophic illness, and sudden loss are all serious problems that will darken the happiest of spirits. You may even feel justified in your unhappiness by accepting the compassion of others for your circumstance. You feel completely comfortable fading into their compassion and sympathies and remaining there without thought. Understand that allowing yourself to remain in this state will also keep you in the darkness. You have a choice as to how long you will allow your spirit to be affected. The amount of time you spend in the darkness should be in direct relation to the seriousness of the event.

Accepting things that you cannot change is another lesson to be learned before we can regain happiness. It is sometimes difficult to recognize when to give up trying to change a situation. I hope this becomes easier now that you are able to listen to your heart. In the quiet reflection the answer may come more easily.

We are already aware and recognize that you cannot change anyone else. Only by being an example of the light within ourselves and being a pebble giving off gentle waves do we allow others the choice to join us in the light. It is each person's choice to change with us or remain the same. Now that we are empowered with the knowledge of who we are, we can better accept others as they are. Knowing that we all have limitations draws us less into their darkness and allows us to remain stronger in the brightness of our spirit. Awareness of our own past darkness may allow a new view into the actions of others.

Accepting and acknowledging when you cannot change a situation is but another one of our choices. You will need to spend time considering if the situation is worth the cost to you. Be aware of the price you pay, in terms of additional effort, time spent and effect on your well being. If you still feel the effort put forth will not be detrimental to your journey, then continue working to change the situation. But remain aware of the toll it takes upon you. You can at any point choose to accept that you cannot change the situation. It is your choice and your right.

Another lesson to be learned when regaining happiness is how and when to emotionally disconnect from situations and people. It is not sufficient to simply disengage from situations and people; you must make a conscious choice to stop. Let me explain. An emotional disconnect is simply pushing the feeling or emotion to the side, pretending you do not care or refusing to acknowledge its affect upon you. It is still lingering in your spirit and will remain there casting shadows. Simply denying or refusing to address it does nothing to remove it from your being. By being aware and allowing the spirit to make a conscience choice will allow it to leave your being. You are free to move on having looked at the situation or person in the full light of your bright spirit.

There is no better time than now for you to be happy. If you wait for all the wrongs to be right, for all circumstances to be perfect, for people to be who you want them to be, happiness will continue to elude you. Since we can only change ourselves and we are responsible for finding and keeping our own happiness that is what we will learn. We make our world happy by being happy ourselves, not by trying to make others around us happy.

Let's look at some of the happiest people in the world and what we may be able to learn from them. Bhutan is a Buddhist village in the Himalayan Mountains with a foundation based on the happiness of its people. Every government decision is weighed with consideration into the effect it will have on the well being of the citizens. While most countries measure the GNP (Gross National Product), Bhutan measures the GNH (Gross National Happiness). It is their belief that regulation and monitoring of outside influences such as tourism, the pace of technological advances, economic development, the effect of changes on the environment and promotion of the heritage and culture will help them retain the level of happiness they now possess. In short they are not willing to compromise happiness for the gain of material possessions and monetary advances. Their government leaders had the foresight to realize that change is inevitable but looked to balance the pace of those changes, and address the influences and their effect upon their citizens.

Now let's look at our lives. Most of us rarely consider the consequences of the choices we make for ourselves and how they impact our happiness. We need to begin including this awareness. Before making decisions we need to view how they will impact our life and happiness and affect the quality of our journey.

So how can we retain the balance of happiness while assessing opportunities? The examples are endless but I have included a few things to consider when viewing your choices.

Technology - it is apparent to me that our spirituality has not kept pace with our technological advances. We have lost the human in humanity. We have become an adversary onto ourselves. Computers keep us captive and captivated. The Internet connects us to all the answers to any question we can come up with. We no longer have a need to ponder the universe because we can now look it up on the Internet. Cell phones keep us in a constant state of connection and conversation. Video games have replaced human contact for our children. These games create a world where they can harm, rob and kill without seeing the human result of their act. All of this occurs in our lives without us being aware of how we are being affected or harmed by technology.

We grow personally and spiritually by reading, learning, and sharing thoughts and ideas. We thrive on human contact and developing relationships that result in the evolution of our consciousness. But go to any coffee shop and you will see people sitting alone engrossed in the events taking place on their laptops. It is much harder to expand our consciousness without enriching dialog. The Internet can provide us with many facts and information but no humanity.

Humans need human contact and we are moving further and further away from that contact. The human component has been removed from so many of our tasks. More and more people work and attend school from home. It is now possible to remain in our house for long periods of time and have all of our needs cared for via delivery or through the Internet. We have even eradicated the need to speak with the advent of sending text messages and emails. Should you need to actually speak to someone do not fear you can attach a phone to your ear so are hands are free to perform other tasks.

In addition, technology is far outpacing morality. Right and wrong and black and white are rigid lines that are drawn with cynicism and skepticism without including the human side of the issue. There are so many ways to monitor and self regulate technology's harmful effects on our spirit. It is of great importance that you become aware, on a daily basis, of how technology isolates you from other humans and the effect it can have on your spirit.

Just say no! Do you recall the *War on Drugs* campaign during the 80's and 90's? We need to bring the slogan back but this time for our well-being. We are unable to say no. We don't think twice about requests that will have a negative effect on our time, resources and health. The toll on our well-being and happiness is dramatic. We allow ourselves to be pulled in different directions with all the demands, opportunities, commitments and responsibilities. I am asking you to become aware the effect not including ***no*** in your answer is having upon your happiness.

Why do we allow ourselves to feeling guilt for saying no? Because our loud ego drowns out the quiet voice trying to be heard. If we say no we may miss something, be left out, and most importantly, we would need to come up with a good excuse for why we said no. You have the right to say no if it is not in the best interest of your well-being and you should feel no need to be drawn in. Replies such as, 'unfortunately it is not possible at this time to'...or 'let me look at my schedule and I will email you', are acceptable. You will find that it is easier if your answer leaves no room for questions or further explanations. Your bright spirit will know how to listen to hear the right answer from within. Trust in yourself that you are now aware and can see the toll always saying yes has on your spirit.

Health - We all understand to be healthy we need to include exercise and be mindful of what we are eating. Health comes from balance. It is a balance that includes exercise but health also comes from your well-being. Stress, tension, anxiety and fear all play a big role in your overall health. Working long hours without including time for exercise or not eating nutritious meals has an impact on your well being. Obesity and medical issues have caused hypertension, diabetes and depression rates to soar. Seventy three percent of Americans state that money is the number one factor in the level of their stress. Is this all worth the price we are paying to have material possessions? We again need to consider our health when making choices. We must take into consideration our entire well-being and happiness in all of our choices.

Monetary Gain - Many times our only consideration in the pursuit of bigger and better is the belief that if we make more money we will be able to have more and better things. We now know through awareness that having more things does not result in more happiness. Remember the poorest people in the world with the least amount of possessions are often the happiest. Remember your gifts of love, peace, gratitude and hopes and dreams are free. They do not cost you anything. You cannot accept change without weighing the cost of its impact on your happiness.

Maybe an opportunity is not as good as it first appears when you look at it in terms of its effect on your entire being. Will it mean less time with family and friends? Will it mean less opportunity to meet new people who may enrich your life in ways you could never imagine? What are you willing to trade for more and bigger? Is it part of the *everything* you are looking for? Often times we admire the people who are willing to sacrifice anything to climb to the top because we do not see the cost. The person who realizes that the quality of their life is more important and turns down an opportunity for advancement should also be admired for their courage or perhaps even more so for taking a stand for what is best for their happiness? I am not saying that you should turn down every promotion or refuse the opportunity to advance your career. What I am saying is that you need to look at the entire view and see if the cost to your well-being is balanced by the opportunity.

You can be aware and reject the proposed changes if they are not what is best for you and your happiness. It will take a spirit bright to see that your authentic self is not what you do, or what you possess. It will take referring back to the things we have learned earlier to determine what is the best choice to make and if any occupant rules need to be in place before accepting the changes. Putting occupant rules in place will force you to keep a balance. You can make a change even if it will have a negative impact but you must demand a balance for its cost. You will determine what the balance is in relation to the cost to your well being. For example, let's say you have additional business travel – you would balance that with a weekend of no work. The same applies if you accepted a promotion at work that creates more stress – it could be balanced with hiring someone to help with housework. Do you understand the point I am making? Balance the effect of the gain with the cost on your spirit and hold to the deal you have made with yourself.

What is the happiness factor? It is the result of scientific research conducted by Robin Sieger that analyzed which factors go into what makes most of us happy. Each of the factors listed will be followed by a direct correlation to changes we have made to enrich our lives and allow happiness to return.

High self-esteem - when we learned to become aware of how others speak to us, and how we speak to ourselves, we grow to understand that we are a gift. And that awareness becomes ingrained into the fabric of our being. In short, we allow our self-esteem to flourish while keeping our ego in check.

Optimism - with the ego put in its place and gratitude now an integral part of our map, we are more aware of our choices. We are moving closer to being brighter in spirit and more optimistic.

Close friendships or satisfying relationships - by removing the people who do not have our best interest at heart or who darken our spirit, we allow space for other more enriching relationships to flourish.

Faith - is ever present in the quiet of our spirit. We will discuss the important part faith plays further in a following chapter.

Sleep & Exercise - realizing that you are a gift to yourself brings to light the importance of treating yourself with love and care. Make better choices for your well being and understand how unhealthy habits impact how you are able to take care of the gift of your being.

The Sieger study also found that the following factors are *not* associated with the level of happiness;

Age
Gender
Education level
Parenthood – having children
Attractiveness – physical

Realize that you have within you the capacity to be happy. Seek its return without placing conditions. Develop a positive attitude and believe that the most important relationship you will have in your life is with yourself.

Let's take our gifts and move forward to find love.

Finding Love

Seeking love in your life only makes it more elusive. The answer to its mysterious gift is to love yourself first and remain open to all possibilities. The love you are looking for may not be delivered in the package you expect, but you may be surprised by the treasure you find once you dare to look inside.

Kim Upstone

You may think finding love is an opportunity for us to look beyond ourselves at the role others play in our relationships. No, it is still all about us. Looking for someone to love is much like finding happiness. Instead of seeking love, allow it to come to you. Be conscious of the light within ourselves and how it draws people to us.

While on this journey we have become adept at being aware and looking honestly at ourselves. We will use these tools again to figure out complicated relationships and what path leads to true love.

Can you feel the light and is it bright and strong in your spirit? Can you feel the calmness within? That calmness allows us to slow down the boat and look for the beauty that surrounds us. There is no longer any reason to look back at the darkness. We have left it behind us. But, with gratitude for having once been in the darkness, we can look with anticipation to the remainder our journey. Our future is bright and filled with an abundance of happiness.

Every step that we have taken to this point will allow us to be open to love entering our life or renewing and strengthening our current relationships. I shared with you earlier that this journey was as important to the people I touch as it was for the people who have touched me and here is where we will see it's truth.

My journey allowed me to free others to be true to their own light. By giving myself the gift of unconditional love I have inadvertently given them the freedom of *not* becoming who I wanted them to be. They no longer needed to live up to what I expected. No proof of love was needed, and no jealousy or requirements and conditions had to be met. They were free to follow their own journey and give love from the depths of their own being. There is no greater love than the love that is given or received without conditions or demands. When you are present in a relationship because you choose to be there, and not out of need, it frees you to look with clarity at the person you choose to be with.

First, let's address why you cannot love another until you first love yourself. If you do not love yourself you will *need* others to fill the darkness within. Your spirit being filled with light by your own happiness allows you to love without expectations, requirements, demands, jealousy and fear. The only time that you are free to love completely is when you are free from conditions and requirements. And it is in your light that you realize real and lasting relationships are created. It is in simplifying that interaction that complicated relationships become clearer.

Love cannot be created in the relationship by one person. It is doomed if built upon need or expectation. This creates a weak foundation that cannot bear the weight of challenges and rough waters. A strong relationship must be built by two people working together in the light. Each person must grow within their own light strong and bright while choosing to grow together to build a strong foundation. There may be times in a relationship that one person will bear the weight alone. During times of darkness you will carry each other. But this imbalance cannot remain so for long if the bond is to remain strong. For love to remain bright, each person must carry their own weight and know what they need to do to keep their own light shining brightly.

In addition, you cannot change anyone but yourself. If you enter into a relationship thinking the other person will become who you want them to be you have created an unrealistic expectation. Because you are creating a condition to be met the expectation will remain unfulfilled; no one should abandon being true to their light to fulfill your expectations. You will be left in darkness wondering why you have never found *the everything* you are seeking. There is no brightness for a person who expects to change someone else to fit the picture created in their mind of the perfect mate. If you look with awareness at the person who is before you and decide that you can be happy with whom they are now then feel free to pursue the relationship. Be aware that you have made a choice within the brightness of your spirit to allow them to be who they want to be.

When you think of the person you love as a gift they become a gift. If you look each day for the goodness within the person you love, you will see goodness. You will see what you are looking for; let it be the good qualities. Loving someone does not mean acceptance of everything they do. Certainly irritations and annoyances and problems will arise in any relationship. Attempting to ignore them and pretend they do not exist will not serve you. Over time they will shadow the light within your spirit. We need to view them in the context of the entirety of the person. Create a balance of negative things you do not like with goodness and kindness you also see. If you spend day after day not looking for the goodness within someone, you will soon forget to look.

Chances are that in your own darkness you have chosen to ignore the good. Looking through your ego's view for things that contradicted the picture of perfection you created in your mind of who they should be, and how they should respond to your needs. Now that you are bright of spirit it is easier for us to give up the demands we placed on them and they are free to be true to their spirit. This is much like the work we have done on ourselves, where we keep reaching for brightness. And so it works the same with others. Once we see goodness in them and show more kindness and forgiveness, the more motivated they seek to become brighter themselves. By loving them without conditions we allow them room to breathe freely without our expectations weighing them down. This change allows for two candles to stand separately, still burning brightly together providing light and illuminating the world.

Let's look at some areas covered earlier, but now we will look with awareness at their impact when we build or strengthen our relationships.

Self-Talk – Along with positive self-talk comes the risk that you allow the ego to slip in and influence the conversation in your mind. Unchecked it can undermine the balance of respect and self-esteem which can darken to become arrogance and superiority. You must be vigilant that your self-talk remains about yourself and your light. Never in any relationship should you compare or rank yourself above or below others. A relationship is mutual and only when you are equal in your mind can you grow together. The minute you allow yourself to think you are better than someone else you disturb the balance allowing the darkness to return.

Negative self-talk will keep you from being an equal in any relationship. The minute you hear the negativity return you will revert to the darkness. Look to address the negativity honestly and in the light. You will instinctively look for a solution or compromise to solve it. Let negativity play a part and you will have allowed ego to overtake the quiet peaceful spirit. Becoming defensive and not be able to view the problem honestly or placing yourself in a position of weakness allows the ego of the other person to overtake you with darkness.

Gratitude-There is nothing quite like gratitude for another person to strengthen a relationship. Having a relationship is a choice and earlier we learned that you have a choice to look at anything with more than one view. And this holds true with our relationships. You can view your relationship with gratitude and see it as a part of *your everything*. Or, you can view it as not enough and see that it adds little to your being. If you can find no gratitude but are simply satisfied with the relationship you are in, you are not moving together towards the light. Renew the passion or purpose to propel the relationship towards the brightness. Gratitude is a great way to renew the passion or purpose for another person. Find the goodness and kindness and believe that they are a gift and your passion may return.

Caution is needed when you are traveling through this part of your journey. Remember to be a pebble and cast yourself gently allowing change to occur slowly. Understand that others who love and care for you may have spent great effort on making you happy during your relationship. Once you are self reliant it may be hard for them to understand that you do not need them to be anyone other than who they are or who they want to become. They may feel empty without your needs to fill their spirit and brighten their light. Give them time; look with kindness and gratitude that they looked to be your light. Look for ways to grow in the light together while building a strong foundation.

Worry- Many times when we allow ourselves the gift of loving someone without conditions, we feel vulnerable and become worrisome. We believe we have given up control when in truth we never had control. No one, with the exception of someone held captive has the ability to control another person. Remember we are responsible for our choices and ourselves. We can think of every scenario and try to change the free will of another but we will still never be able to control the outcome. The ego tricks us into believing we have power over the outcome and then fills our spirit with darkness when we realize we are powerless against the outcome. Nothing takes the power of worry away quite like a spirit strong and bright - it is your best defense against worry.

What ifs - The questions are endless. It is true that love can hurt and the subsequent pain can darken the lives of some for the rest of their journey. Remember it is your choice to remain in the darkness. It may be painful but spend a little time, view it in the light, and be realistic about the part you played. Don't spend one moment trying to figure out the other part of the equation – because you never will figure out someone else's thinking. Looking back does nothing to move you forward. As long as you can be sure your ego, or placing conditions on that person, did not play a role in the relationship then move on. It may sound cold and heartless but when you love yourself and view the relationship realistically, you may understand that the gift that you would have brought to the relationship may not have been a good fit for the other person. People are sometimes more fearful of light than darkness. It is possible your light was just too bright! Move on and find someone who appreciates the bright and wants to work to join you in building a strong foundation.

Our lack of communication is apparent to me as it becomes harder and harder to keep communications foremost in our relationships. Technology continues to inhibit real communications. We send emails and texts more easily than actually speaking. We spend endless hours on the Internet looking for ideal partners. I cannot comprehend the joy in putting in an order for someone to love. I am sure there are success stories, but my belief is that most people are not truthful about the information they are submitting. Being untruthful is not a good way to begin a new relationship.

How much communication is then required to establish trust after untruths? We are humans and we require human contact. I have often heard that people do not have the time to invest in finding someone. If you find that this is the case, please go back and read Happiness again and focus on the monetary gain vs. your happiness section. Relationships are created by the exchange of ideas and sharing views and thoughts. It is within those exchanges that we can see the light, the goodness, the kindness of another, and that helps us decide if we choose to move forward or move on. It is in the light of another that we choose to give the gift of ourselves.

Labels- when finding love we often put conditions and requirements on whom we choose to be with. We need to remove preconceived notions and labels and remain open to anyone we meet. Your gift may not come in the package you expect but if you dare to ignore the wrapping you may find a wondrous gift is inside. Happiness lies in the spirit, not in the rank you give another and you cannot view another person's spirit from afar. You must take the risk, get close and view it in the light. You need to look deep and look for the light within another. Then and only then can you choose to do the work and be the pebble that sends out gentle waves to brighten someone's light by revealing your own.

Darkness in relationships – As your spirit becomes brighter it becomes more difficult to stay in a relationship that is dark and harmful to your spirit. Looking at the relationship after you have made changes to yourself may give you a clearer picture. Be wary of being drawn back into the darkness. Other people's egos are involved and they may take every opportunity to engage you in their struggle to keep you from who you want to become.

Becoming aware of a relationship that is not good for your well-being is very hard. Knowing when to let go and end a relationship is difficult, because it requires us to give up something that was created to fill an empty spot inside. Giving up means that the perfect scenario we have in our mind will never be fulfilled. A test of our brightness and an understanding of the need to remain in the light of our spirit will undoubtedly reveal itself when we become aware that a relationship is ending. It is a patch of rough water on the river that we have prepared for. Just holding onto until the water becomes smooth again is not enough.

Don't allow yourself to throw down the anchor and remain stagnant. Treat yourself kindly and remind yourself of your map, and continue on your journey into the light. Remember that the end of one relationship does not signal the beginning of another. You can be perfectly content alone now. Do not close yourself off to opportunities but do not force the situation. Allow the space that has opened up within your spirit to remain open for a bit. Allow the light to regain brightness before allowing another attempt. Filling the space quickly may feel right but that is not the direction we need to grow in. You need to take the time needed to become strong of spirit again.

Dark of Spirit and light stealers - there are times that you may choose to stop rowing against the flow of the river and abandon the relationship you are in. This is especially true when you realize that you are in a relationship with a person who has a very dark of spirit or is a light stealer. Understand that you cannot make a relationship work with these people unless they choose to make a drastic change. You may have entered into the relationship at a time when your own spirit was dark or you were unaware that they were of a dark spirit. In the brightness you can see their true darkness and you have a choice to make. Everyone has the right to refuse to be treated poorly or disrespected. Any abuse, whether mental or physical, is unacceptable. If you find yourself in this situation seek help. Every living being deserves a life free from any type of abuse. Please find someone to help you remain safe.

Much of our beliefs about relationships and how they function came as a result of observing our parents, friends and from our own past experiences. Some of us even believe we can recreate relationships we see on television. The current trend is to have a television show openly illustrate dysfunctional relationships. Even worse are the vast assortment of reality shows where relationships implode before our eyes. Our egos are drawn to the drama created by watching others and their difficult struggles. Others may glean their ideas about relationships from novels and believe that love should be like a story in a book. The reality is that love and relationships are nothing like these examples. Love is created by two people working together and choosing to develop and nurture their relationship. Each relationship is different than any other and there is no right or wrong. If both people feel respected and loved and no one is hurt, then that is a relationship built on a solid foundation of truth and will have a better opportunity for success.

Let's look at a few questions to help us define the way we view relationships. We need to understand which views we may need to change in order to create a lasting and loving relationship.

Please take your journal out and find the peaceful place within that is speaking to you softly. When you have found that place write down your thoughts for each question below.

1) Do I see the role self-talk plays in my relationships?
2) Can I see how gratitude will change how I view my relationship?
3) How does discarding worry allow me to focus better on building a strong relationship?

4) *Can I clearly see the benefit of spending time together, free of distractions?*
5) *Do I agree that labels and conditions may keep me from discovering a gift?*
6) *Do I understand that I need to remove them from my life if I am ever to find a fulfilling relationship?*
7) *Do I see my current relationship with clarity whether dark or light? Do I know that decisions made need to be based on two people being equal in the relationship?*

Together, let's create some guidelines you can look to for your current or any new relationships. Take out your journal again and write some thoughts on our new awareness using the answers to the questions above to guide you. Use the examples below for ideas to help you determine your true feelings. Write out your thoughts and awareness before the occasion arises so that you may refer back to the rules you have created for yourself. Keep in mind that this is no place for the ego's arrogance. Do not compare and do not label. Simply set standards for yourself. To remain bright of spirit we must demand that we be treated with respect and according to the rules we have set up for ourselves.

1) I am not to create conditions but the following things I will not tolerate. List those things!
2) I will remove myself immediately from any relationship, for my own well-being and safety if I view any of the following. Make your list. After removing myself to a safe place I will then look with clarity and decide if the relationship should continue.
3) I will do the following to remain bright in the light of my spirit so that I can be a strong part of the foundation of a healthy and happy relationship. List the things.
4) When disagreements occur, and before the darkness of anger and criticism erupts, I will seek the calm that lies within. I will not darken the light and weaken the foundation with the egos hurtful words and ways.
5) I will define each difference or problem as they appear and not allow myself to "lump" all small problems together. I will realize that a series of small problems are not indicative of a bad relationship but part of the entirety of the relationship.
6) I will realize and look to embrace the many ways there are to show love for another. I will strive to look at the complete view of a person's actions

> *instead of my preconceived notions to determine if love is present.*
> 7) *When a complaint arises I will work to revise it to a question looking for a solution instead of just reinforcing the problem in my mind.*

I believe with awareness and focus you will find a loving relationship built upon admiration and respect for one another. You will have a relationship not built on perfection and conditions, but created on a foundation of shared hopes and dreams. A healthy relationship is a wonderful gift that you will look upon each day with gratitude as it becomes a part of the *everything* you are looking for.

Leaving love with our guidelines and awareness we look next to find faith in every step of our journey.

Faith

"Faith is taking the first step even when you don't see the whole staircase".
Martin Luther King Jr.

Are you amazed at the distance we have traveled together? Your faith in me has allowed you to alter your life and take step after step without seeing the entire staircase. You trusted that I would lead you toward the light and away from darkness. You had the faith not only to dip your foot in the water but submerse yourself. You have worked hard to get to this point in our journey and that work has allowed you to make changes in your life that will be your companion to the end of your journey. You now know how to keep vigilant and remain in the light, peaceful and content with happiness and brightness in your spirit.

Let's now look at faith and the part it plays in *our everything*. I have saved faith for last believing that had I included my personal beliefs early in our journey that those who have strong religious beliefs different from mine may be less open to embrace the ideas and the transformations of the entire journey. You now know we can have differences and still be in the light of love, peace and contentment together. I believe that my faith guides me in the brightness. Ego and darkness will lead you to look at religious differences while a spirit bright will lead you to our similarities. Now that your spirit is bright and strong you may be able to look at our differences in a more open and less judgmental light.

Faith, religion and spirituality may all have very different meanings for each of us as we apply them to our life and journey. By understanding that there is no right or perfect way to apply these beliefs in your life we can seek to determine our own meaning and how it is ingrained into our being. What is important is that you look deeply at your own beliefs and allow them to accompany you on your journey. We must look at each faith, religion and spirituality individually as well as together and understand the influence they have on our journey.

I believe faith is personal for each of us. Faith is a belief and trust in something or someone that remains unproven. Faith is within everyone but it is the depth of faith and what we place our faith in that creates differences in our belief systems. Even people who do not believe in a higher power still have faith that there is no higher power. All religions are based in faith. Opposing religions are even based in faith. Each group of followers believes that their faith is correct. Faith without awareness can lead to false belief and blind faith can lead you to darkness. It is not about wrong or right. Our higher power created faith to allow each of us the ability to believe, but what we believe in, is left up to each of us. Be aware that yours is faith with awareness knowing that we each have the right to our own faith, as long as no harm is done to another and without judgment of right or wrong.

Religion is a group of people who are guided by a common belief system. It is within that group that rules and guidelines are formed. Some people in certain regions of the world are persecuted if they choose a religion different than that of their family, neighbors and ethnicity. Each of us must remain aware that the group that you are in reflects the beliefs that whisper within your heart. If at any time you feel your religion no longer reflects your beliefs and you feel the direction it is taking you is not true your heart, than you need to look at if your religion is truly serving you. Just as each of us have a different passion and purpose that allows our spirit to remain bright; it is the same when seeking a religion. You must seek your truth within your own heart. Along with faith and spirituality, our higher power provides us with religious choice. Do not follow anything that your feel in your heart is hurtful or harmful to others and is shrouded in darkness. Man creates and, in some cases, manipulates religion for his own use. So use caution and awareness that the religion you choose is what you truly feel in your heart.

Spirituality is a personal connection with your higher power. It is working to find the place within us that is peaceful, calm and quiet.

It is here that we find our truths and can become who we need to be. It is within our spirituality that our ego withdraws and we see our purpose with clarity. It is with faith that we are able to take our journey, making our way through the darkness to the light and revealing our purpose. When we are bright of spirit, and possess calmness and peace in our hearts then we can see ourselves as one with the world. A relentless spirit is always seeking to understand and grow, fascinated by the amazing beauty and empowering choices offered for our taking.

I know when I said it is all about you earlier a number of you thought instantly I cannot be most important in my life. You may have thought - God, my higher power, my maker is always first. This is where our beliefs may differ slightly. I believe that I cannot love God freely and completely until I first love myself. By being strong and bright I can then come to him with unfaltering love and faith. It is when our relationship with him is built upon need with conditions and requirements that our darkness returns. It is in the darkness we look to him to be the light for us. However, he has given each of us our own light so that we may seek our own brightness and shine in unity with his light. Once bright we help him light the darkness of the world.

It is with gratitude for his unwavering love for me, that I can build a strong foundation much like the relationship of love but this time the relationship is with my maker. It is my belief that we are created of the light from within the maker's own spirit and I, like each of us, came forth as a gift from him. This is a gift of life that was given out of his pure love for us.

Each and every one of us has a purpose and it is within our journey and finding the light within that our purpose is revealed. In accepting that you are a gift you will recognize and be truly grateful for that gift. And when you are your brightest you will understand and hear your purpose, in your heart. You will see the light within yourself and learn to keep it bright by being true to who you are to become. You will leave conditions and requirements in the darkness as you move toward his light and closer to his infinite love.

Even though the maker is a constant, our understanding of him and our purpose will evolve as we travel on our journey. Our awareness and comprehension of him is never stagnant but ever evolving. We must not stop learning and growing. He does not ask us to martyr ourselves but seeks for us to live in the light. And during times of darkness and despair he will carry us, but after every moment of darkness he is close by offering his own light to light the path. I believe his wish is that we again reclaim our light and walk *with* him once again. He does not wish us to remain in the darkness but to find the strength to once again regain the brightness of our spirit and the infinite power it holds.

We all came to this journey as distinctive human beings, with varied and diverse backgrounds, and we will leave this journey as distinctive human beings. It is right that we remain in our own uniqueness. Through my eyes, in the brightness of my spirit I see our similarities and honor our differences. I believe that those differences allow us an opportunity to grow and learn from each other. If we could just look for the light within each spirit we would realize that within our spirit we are all created the same.

Let's walk in the light towards the end of this journey together.

The End But Never Done

I have guided your steps through this journey, but it is you who must choose to continue moving your feet.
                                            Kim Upstone

As we are approaching the end of this part of your transformation, and our journey together, I hope that I have led you to a place within yourself that you never dreamed existed. That the work you have done has allowed you to discover what I know to be true in my heart. That everything begins with you.

I hope you now understand more fully who you are, and with new awareness see that you are well on your way to finding *your everything*. You can now move forward in the world with clarity and an understanding of the power you possess. Know in your heart that you truly are a gift - a gift to be cherished. Move through each moment aware of the beauty within you and that which surrounds you.

I hope that you now understand the importance of being able to dance in the storm because you recognize that life is too precious to keep waiting for the storm to pass. I hope you realize that we cannot stop the waves from pushing you down the river but with awareness and choice you can slow down, look at the beauty all around you and arrive at the end of your journey with the light within your spirit bright and strong.

I hope you realize that you like me, a lovely rose bud that is now blooming into a beautiful flower. As each petal withers and falls it will only serve to remind you that we are all given a limited time for our journey. But with each falling petal we need not fear the demise of the flower but look to embrace each moment of its beautiful existence while it is with us.

I hope that you live generously unto yourself and are lovingly guided by gratitude and love in your spirit. I hope that you see your awakening as a treasure you will count among the other gifts you are eternally grateful for.

I hope that you now know who you are. Realize you are a gift to be cherished. Do you now feel that you are one with the light in your spirit and the voice in your heart? Are you love, joy and happiness? Do you realize that these gifts were already within you? They were being kept safe until you became aware and chose to bring them into the light.

I hope you now feel strong and understand that you do not need others to reinforce who you are. You do not require acknowledgement or admiration from anyone. Instead you can now look deep inside to receive direction for your choices. Be true to your heart and allow the light within to guide you.

I hope that you have discovered that *your everything* is that which already lies in the brightness of your spirit and the depth of love within your heart.

I hope you will clearly see my purpose for writing this book and my passion for showing you the path to your happiness. Even though this journey is about each of us individually growing in the light, we are all connected, each of us to another. We must use each moment we are alive to be the light that may change the darkness of the world.

I hope that each day you will show kindness to at least one person you might normally have not noticed before. With the gift of your spirit bright you will now see through eyes of compassion and be compelled to be aware of the great need and help those who are placed in your path. They are sent to you for a reason, you must not look away. You may find all that is needed is a smile or kind word. You may be called to give of your time or share in the abundance of your gifts. When you are able to give of yourself and ask nothing in return, then you will know you are being true to your spirit and honoring the gift that was given when you were created.

I hope you understand that you were guided to take this journey with me and that all is as it should be. You are now where you were meant to be, in the light.

Every day of my life I will look with gratitude, touched that you have chosen to accept the awareness of the light. Every day I pray that my message will reach others also seeking enlightenment.

I believe inside all of our spirits lies the answer to our existence and that of the entire world. The light that shines brightly within us is bright by choice. The choices each of us makes to find and allow it to be our guide is the reason each of us has been given the gift to be here. If everyone in the world was guided by the light within their spirit, our world would be a much different place. By each of us living everyday in the light of a bright spirit and by lighting the way for others remaining in darkness, we can work together to make the world a place of peace and unity.

The entire world would realize the power of living each day with…

> *…**love** for all and be able to truly love everyone including themselves without restrictions.*
>
> *…**grace** with gentleness towards others and acceptance of their limitations.*
>
> *…and **gratitude** for everything we have been given.*

"A life is like a piece of paper on which everyone leaves their mark"

Chinese Proverb

My wish when we began this journey together was that the mark I would leave on your piece of paper would be one that you would carry with you in the brightness of your spirit to the end of your journey. I hope that this has happened and I have empowered you to seek and share happiness. But what has become even more clear is the mark that taking this journey with you has left on my piece of paper, stained with tears of happiness that I do not believe will ever dry. I believe that it has fulfilled my purpose for being here and for that I will be forever grateful to each of you.

The End But Never Done

We will meet again at the end of the river, bathed in the glow of all the love we have given and all the love we have received. Happiness radiates from each of us, and the light of all our spirits unite to light the path for others to follow.

Namaste

Made in the USA
Charleston, SC
01 December 2009